# BOSTON
## —— IN THE ——
# AMERICAN REVOLUTION

# BOSTON

## — IN THE —

# AMERICAN REVOLUTION

## A TOWN VERSUS AN EMPIRE

BROOKE BARBIER

*Foreword by Alan Taylor*

THE
History
PRESS

Published by The History Press
Charleston, SC
www.historypress.net

Copyright © 2017 by Brooke Barbier
All rights reserved

First published 2017

Manufactured in the United States

ISBN 9781467135887

Library of Congress Control Number: 2016947533

*To Cheryl & Jack*

# CONTENTS

# CONTENTS

# FOREWORD

I began my career as a historian in Boston, where I often could walk about to see famous sites from the American Revolution. Later, I moved across the continent to a university in California, where I found a surprising number of students keen to know more about the nation's origins in seaport cities of the Atlantic seaboard. Among them, Brooke Barbier stood out as intellectually curious and infectiously enthusiastic. In pursuit of her passion, Brooke moved to Boston to pursue graduate study, work in publishing and develop her own tours of the city's historic landscape. She has acquired a great love for the city, deep knowledge of its past and a rare talent for explaining history. Her expertise and devotion illuminate every page of this insightful and lively exploration of the revolution in the city where it began. As I read these pages, she becomes my guide to a history that has become her own. I especially recommend this book to readers seeking to know more about the social and political context of the intriguing old buildings that invite us to imagine the struggles of a now-distant century.

—Alan Taylor
Thomas Jefferson Foundation Chair
University of Virginia

# Acknowledgements

I want to first thank all of the guests who have joined me on Ye Olde Tavern Tours. Your deep curiosity and interest in the lesser-known stories about Boston during the American Revolution motivated me to write this book.

As the research for this book is based mostly on secondary sources, I thank the historians and writers who have written before me whose scholarship, coverage of Boston's history or exquisite writing inspired me. These include, but are not limited to, Robert Allison, Charles Bahne, Bernard Bailyn, Benjamin Carp, David Hackett Fischer, Esther Forbes, Edmund S. Morgan, Nathaniel Philbrick, Annie Haven Thwing, Gordon Wood and Alfred F. Young. I am also indebted to scholar J.L. Bell, whose meticulously researched blog, *Boston 1775*, is a place to get lost for an afternoon. Most of all, though, I thank Alan Taylor for being a source of inspiration and awe to me for nearly two decades. His American Revolution class at the University of California, Davis motivated my first trip to Boston and exploration of the Freedom Trail. Not only is he an exceptional teacher, but he is also one of the top scholars in the country. It's not just me who says so—he has won two Pulitzer Prizes in history. I admire him unceasingly and was honored that he agreed to write the foreword for this book.

I thank several institutions simply for being. Their very existence makes Boston a rich center for visitors, residents, schoolchildren and scholars to study and appreciate history. These include the Boston Athenaeum, Boston National Historical Park, Boston Public Library, Freedom Trail Foundation,

Massachusetts Historical Society and Paul Revere Memorial Association. I am especially grateful to the Bostonian Society for maintaining the most impressive building in the city, the Old State House, and have appreciated its collaboration in the past. My gratitude also extends outside Massachusetts to the New York Public Library, the Smithsonian Institute and the Library of Congress.

I thank the librarians and research specialists who helped me gain access to some of the incredible images you'll find throughout this book, including Martina Beccari at the Museum of Fine Arts, Boston; Jaclyn Penny with the American Antiquarian Society, who was especially heroic in tracking down images; Elizabeth Roscio at the Bostonian Society; Deb Sisum at the National Portrait Gallery, Smithsonian Institution; and Catherine Wood at the Norman B. Leventhal Map Center, Boston Public Library.

Grub Street is a nonprofit writing center in Boston that helped me in the early stages of conceiving and mapping out this book. Teachers Katrin Schumann and Kevin Birmingham exceeded my expectations with their preparation and insight.

I am grateful to the team at The History Press for their work to transform my words into a book. Edward Mack was patient, communicative and helpful, all of which are wonderful qualities for an editor to have, and Abigail Fleming deftly helped me with the details of publication.

I thank my friends, who are spread from California to Boston, for their untiring support and enthusiasm. I especially acknowledge Sarah Nytroe, Ann West and Katie Coaster for reading various versions of my work and providing constructive feedback and cheerful encouragement to keep going. The Clios, Kristen and Nina, helped free up my schedule to write and edit by expertly giving tours. Two dear friends, Markus and Colleen, heard a lot about the process of writing this book and were always ready to have a beer and listen.

Finally, I acknowledge my family. To Danny, Briana and Matt, thank you for supporting my love of books, dating all the way back to you patronizing my library. Jessica and Wes, if you knew me then, I know that you would have supported my library, too. My dad passed on his interest in history to me, and I know that if he were alive today, he'd be the first person to finish reading this book. To my mom, whose enthusiasm and support is limitless, thank you for your mighty love. And to Adam: You are patient, hilarious and forever willing to let me be me. I am so grateful.

# INTRODUCTION

T his book tells the story of how individuals in Boston reacted during an exceptional political and economic crisis lasting from 1763 to 1776. This is not a story about the people of Boston fighting for independence from the British Empire, as the colonists weren't actually seeking to be independent for the vast majority of those years. The men in this story did not have a master plan to become the United States of America or even to split from the British Empire. It is easy to presume that they had such a plan when you know the end of the story, as you inevitably do with the American Revolution. (Spoiler alert: the colonists break free from the mother country.)

When reading this book, we must do our best to forget how the struggle ends because it takes away from the drama. If you already knew how it all turned out (and I ruined that a couple of sentences ago), you'd miss the absolute improvisation and uncertainty surrounding the events you've known about since grade school. When our story begins in 1763, Boston is not a town eager to declare independence or fight in another war; rather, it is an economically depressed postwar town. The French and Indian War had just concluded, and thousands of men from Massachusetts had fought alongside the British as their allies. After the war, many colonists felt proud to be a part of the seemingly successful and ever-expanding British Empire. They weren't longing to split from it.

Instead of viewing the American Revolution as inevitable, I see it as a slow burn, with one event or offense building on another, and one that could have happened differently, even up to the moment of war. As a result, this story does not privilege one event as being more important or revolutionary than another. Some historians claim that a single episode marked the beginning of the American Revolution—the Boston Massacre or the Boston Tea Party, for example—but that is a reductionist view that comes only with the benefit of hindsight. Six weeks before the Boston Tea Party took place, the rebels were not planning to destroy the king's tea. Even a few hours beforehand, the rebels were trying to find a passive, nondestructive way to solve the problem of the tea. They weren't thinking as they dumped tea into the harbor, "This is where we finally sever ties with the British Empire." The United States didn't officially break from the British Empire until it declared independence, and it only stuck after it won an eight-year-long war.

We also must not see the people in this story—even those whom we think we know—as one-dimensional characters with a singular political focus. They were messier and more complicated than that. Please meet them anew on these pages and form new thoughts about them. Just like humans today, human beings in the eighteenth century could be petty, hypocritical and selfish and also hopeful, loving and funny, and you'll see that on these pages. Each chapter highlights a man, or key player, in Boston and the many aspects of his personality. Some remained loyal to the Crown, and some rebelled against British policies. Some have been forgotten and some enshrined in the pantheon of American history. But in this story, none of them are heroes and none of them are villains, even if they were considered as such by their contemporaries.

As the title of this book—*Boston in the American Revolution*—indicates, I unapologetically place Boston at the center of the American Revolution. This is because most of the significant action leading up to war with the British Empire happened in Boston. New York City didn't have the fervent rebel leaders that Boston did or the deep-seated hatred of some of the royal officials ruling their colony, and Philadelphia was far too conservative. Virginia was politically radical but did not have the same men on the street who could intimidate and threaten. Tiny Rhode Island rivaled Boston in its creativity when mobbing but not consistently enough. It truly was Boston's American Revolution.

A note about terminology in this book: I refer to the people who rebelled against the British Crown and its policies as "rebels." It is an imperfect term but better than the sweeping "colonists," which generalizes political sentiment, or the politically charged "Patriots," which they only are to us today because the United States won the war. Had the British Empire prevailed, those we refer to as Patriots would be called traitors. Therefore, I find the best term to be rebels, since that noun is also the verb that best defines their behavior in this book. Those colonists who remained loyal to the Crown are appropriately referred to as "Loyalists," which included Crown officials and ordinary colonists who sided with the British Empire. When reading the voices of rebels and Loyalists, you'll see that I have kept their original eighteenth-century spelling and syntax, which could often be inconsistent and awkward.

Finally, for those who want to take their understanding of Boston's American Revolution to the physical world or visit lesser-known spots off the Freedom Trail, there is the "From Past to Present" feature at the end of each chapter. It provides information about the sites mentioned in that chapter and what they look like today. I founded my tour company in 2013 and have been leading tours of the Freedom Trail since then. I know that visitors to Boston often want to have more context for the historic sites they're visiting. If a trip to Boston isn't in your near future, you can watch short videos online (www.yeoldetaverntours.com/videos) that I have created about many of the sites and people in this book. I hope this book inspires you to continue to learn more about the history of Boston and the people who resided within it.

# 1

# WELCOME TO BOSTON, 1763

*Key Player: Samuel Adams, a Man Ready to Emerge*

I t mattered whether you came by land or by sea if you were going to be impressed by your first glance of Boston. By sea, no question, you'd be charmed by the city's shoreline filled with church steeples and excited by its vast and bustling wharves. By land, not as much. The only land route in and out of Boston was the Neck, a narrow strip about fifty yards wide that sometimes flooded in the spring, turning Boston into a temporary island. So arriving by the Neck meant your journey might be a perilous one, and you'd be rewarded with a vista of gallows and grazing cows and not much else. It also mattered where you came from. If from the countryside, the noise, people and buildings might awe or excite you. If from Europe, you'd likely be disappointed, if not disgusted, by Boston's provincialism. Boston's population of about 15,500 people would seem trifling compared to the nearly 1 million people packed into London. More than anything, though, it mattered when you arrived in Boston.

Because if you arrived in 1763, you'd be shocked. You'd heard that Boston was a town dependent on its busy harbor. One contemporary described Boston Harbor this way: "The Masts of Ships here, and at proper Seasons of the Year, make a kind of Wood of Trees." Where you thought you'd see plentiful ships and a buzz of activity, you'd instead find a fairly quiet harbor. You wouldn't see a forest of ship masts. And the many men it took to make such a harbor hum wouldn't be as visible as you expected. Men in Boston could work as merchants, sailors and fishermen—all jobs dependent on business at sea. Longshoremen loaded and unloaded goods from the ships and docks. Rope workers had the backbreaking job of creating rope to be used aboard the ships, work that required using clubs to beat the rope tightly. Mast builders created ship masts, something for which New England was well known due to its abundance of tall and wide trees. Merchants imported and exported goods and were at the top of the economic pyramid, employing many men to prepare their ships for sea. But now, many merchants in Boston were struggling financially, so the varied men they usually employed had less work or no work at all.[1]

Much of Boston's economy was dependent on labor, goods and money outside of the town because Boston didn't manufacture much—aside from rum, rope and barrels. When times were tough, as they were in 1763, some men and their families needed to move to find work. Poor relief in Boston had increased nearly two and a half times in the last ten years, as people struggled to make ends meet. Maybe it was better there weren't that many men milling about. You'd heard rumblings that smallpox—a highly infectious and deadly disease—was making its way through Boston.

And it wasn't just Boston that was suffering. Its mother country—Great Britain—had just concluded a long and costly war. The French and Indian War, also known as the Seven Years' War by Europeans, began in 1754 and, despite its name, lasted nine years. The British fought to extend their territory in North America and prevent the French Empire from encroaching on

In this view of Boston from the harbor, Long Wharf is visible in the center and, behind it, a quaint skyline of hills and church steeples. *Library of Congress.*

their trade and settlement. Both the British and the French tried to enlist the Native Americans to their sides, but individual tribes allied with whomever was most advantageous to their interests at the time—usually the French. The colonists throughout North America joined the British side and fought alongside the regulars of the British army.

Of all the colonies to fight in the French and Indian War, Massachusetts contributed the most soldiers. Over one-third of the eligible fighting men from Massachusetts participated. These men weren't serving alongside the British army because they believed in the economic goals of the empire—they were making a financial decision. Beginning in 1758, the Crown agreed to pay the soldiers—at a generous rate—and men signed up in droves. This left Massachusetts dependent on Great Britain for payments, but the mother country was essentially insolvent.

After the British won the French and Indian War, the empire was in crippling postwar debt. The national debt of £72 million at the beginning of the war had nearly doubled by 1763 to £122 million. The British were also left with an empire so vast—it now extended west of the Appalachians—that they couldn't possibly control all of it. As commander in chief of British forces in North America, General Thomas Gage had lots of new territory in the West, but he lacked the resources to manage it effectively. An estimated ten thousand troops would be necessary to guard their newly won territory. The Crown couldn't afford to pay for that many troops without help from its colonies—the very people who had just finished fighting a war. So the financial problems of the mother country were soon going to trickle down to its colonies, just as the financial struggles of Boston's merchants trickled down to their workers. But as troubling as Boston might seem, don't turn around just yet. Boston has plenty of alcohol to offer, which you'll likely want after your long journey.

# WELCOME TO BOSTON

Boston in 1763 was a town of less than a thousand acres and a little longer than two miles from tip to tip, vastly smaller than it is today. In eighteenth-century Boston, you could be nearly anywhere in town and smell the salt air. If you entered Boston via the Neck (as long as it was passable), you'd follow Orange Street into town. Once past the desolate Neck, you'd be glad to discover the thoroughfare filled with taverns, where you'd find inexpensive rum, a place to sleep and a place to stable your horse. Orange Street led into the South End of Boston, which was the largest part of town. Some familiar men lived here, including Samuel Adams and Benjamin Franklin, when he was young. The South End was bordered by Boston Common, a nearly fifty-acre park for more cows to graze, residents to enjoy a stroll and carriages to ride through. Boston Common eventually rose to Beacon Hill—the tallest hill in Boston. Beacon Hill earned its name from the beacon that capped it. It was a wooden post whose top would be lit on fire to warn Boston and surrounding towns of danger. Beacon Hill was sparsely settled, except for some houses and ropewalks. The few houses there were stately, including one at the top of the hill. It was one of only four stone mansions in Boston—the residence of Thomas Hancock, uncle of John Hancock.

The center of town was King Street, which began with the Old State House—called the Towne House by contemporaries—and extended down to Long Wharf. Unlike many of the other streets in Boston, King Street was fairly wide and straight. The aptly named Long Wharf was an extension of King Street and stretched for a third of a mile into Boston Harbor. Wealthy merchants—including the hotheaded future troublemaker Richard Clarke—often located their warehouses and offices where King Street met Long Wharf. Some Bostonians even lived on Long Wharf, including portrait artist John Singleton Copley when he was a young boy. In addition to the Old State House, King Street also boasted a courthouse, a customs house and several taverns, inns and shops. A short walk from the Old State House was Faneuil Hall, which functioned as a marketplace on the bottom floor and a town hall on the top. Faneuil Hall sat in the middle of Dock Square, which also had a large market, filled with stalls and small pushcarts. At the edge of Dock Square was Union Street, which would lead a visitor into the North End, passing one of the largest taverns in Boston, the Green Dragon. (A more lustful visitor could take Ann Street to the North End, passing brothels and plenty of prostitutes.)

Boston's oldest and most crowded neighborhood was the North End, and it housed diverse residents. Sailors and artisans, like Paul Revere, lived and worked here, as did families of privilege, including that of Thomas Hutchinson, lieutenant governor of Massachusetts. Most houses in the eighteenth century—and there were about 1,700 of them in Boston—were small, crowded and made of wood and sometimes had a large group of people living there, including children, in-laws, servants

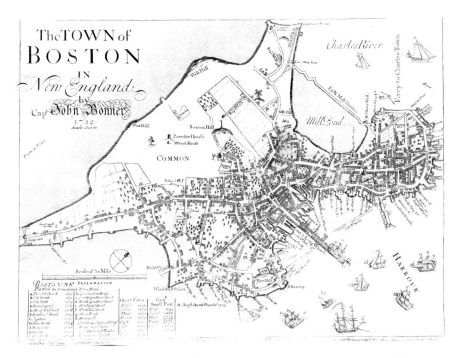

John Bonner's map of Boston in 1722 depicts the vast Common, the crowded North End and Boston's many wharves. *Courtesy of the Norman B. Leventhal Map Center at the Boston Public Library.*

and apprentices. This was especially true in the North End, which also had plenty of warehouses, shops and distilleries. This part of town also boasted the largest cemetery in Boston: the North Burial Ground—known today as Copp's Hill Burying Ground, after the hill it sits on. At the edge of the North End, you'd find Mill Pond, but that wasn't much to look at.

Once you'd learned the town's layout, you'd likely want to entertain yourself in a tavern. Mercifully, Boston had no shortage of alcohol or taverns, serving up cod and baked beans to eat and beer, cider and rum to drink. Hanging out in a tavern would help you to understand the current mood of Boston, as taverns were a place for men to talk about the latest politics. What it lacked in size, population and industry, Boston made up for in opinions. The town had exemplary schools and several bookstores, and Massachusetts boasted a higher literacy rate than those of England and other North American colonies. In the 1760s and '70s, Boston typically had five different newspapers operating—all of which lacked the neutrality some newspapers strive for today—while a similarly sized town in England printed just one. Those newspapers were often read aloud in taverns, and then patrons discussed (or argued about) the news out of London and other colonies. Recently, the reports out of London hadn't been good.

# "IMPROVING THE REVENUE OF THIS KINGDOM"

George Grenville, prime minister of Great Britain since April 1763, had been tasked with managing Great Britain's budget after the French and Indian War, which was no small job given its immense debt. He decided he could make an immediate impact if he squeezed money out of the North American colonies. One way to do that was to reduce smuggling. Peter Oliver, a member of a prominent Loyalist family who wrote a scathing history of the American Revolution in 1781, said that the people of Massachusetts were "notorious in the smuggling Business," with everyone participating, from "the Capital Merchant down to the meanest Mechanick." Grenville's task was to develop a plan to get even the meanest mechanics to start paying customs duties. It wasn't the first time that Parliament—Great Britain's legislative body—had tried to raise revenue by cutting down on smuggling. It had spent the last thirty years trying to tax a popularly imported good.[2]

On the books since 1733, the Molasses Act taxed foreign molasses imported into the colonies. Rum—made from molasses—was a thriving industry in Massachusetts, with over sixty distillers producing nearly three million gallons of rum annually. If the colonists actually paid the required tax on molasses, it would have been a significant source of revenue for Britain. Problematically for the Crown, greedy customs officers could be easily bought off for much less than the cost of the tax, miraculously transforming molasses imported from French Caribbean islands into molasses from the British West Indies. This practice existed for long enough that men in Boston and Massachusetts seemed to think it was their right to avoid paying taxes.

Grenville's solution to the empire's debt and the moribund Molasses Act was the American Duties Act, passed in 1764. It was widely known as the Sugar Act because one of the act's components was a three-penny tax on foreign molasses. The act claimed that "new provisions and regulations should be established for improving the revenue of this kingdom" and for "defraying the expences of defending, protecting, and securing the same." And unlike the Molasses Act,

A self-satisfied George Grenville. *The Miriam and Ira D. Wallach Division of Art, Prints and Photographs: Print Collection, New York Public Library.*

the Sugar Act actually had the necessary muscle to be enforced. Under the new law, the British navy was now empowered to seize any ship believed to skirt paying its taxes. A portion of the contraband went to the customs officer who seized the haul, greatly incentivizing them to capture more ships.[3]

Grenville had no illusion that his Sugar Act would greatly diminish the hefty national debt or pay for all of the troops stationed throughout North America, but he felt that the colonists needed to pay a portion of the expenses to maintain the colonies and their safety. After minimal debate, Parliament passed Grenville's Sugar Act. In doing so, Parliament ignored the fact that the people of Massachusetts had been living on their own for nearly a century and a half, governing and taxing themselves with very little interference from the Crown. Consequently, colonists in Massachusetts felt entitled to self-rule and didn't want to be told where their money had to go—especially after they had just fought in a war to benefit the British Empire and were in severe economic trouble themselves. The idea of self-rule made sense in Boston and Massachusetts, where politics—as they usually are—were local. The towns in Massachusetts were mostly autonomous, conducting their own town meetings, which dealt almost exclusively with local matters. Such town meetings had been around since the seventeenth century, so men in Massachusetts grew up having a say in their government. The town meetings derived from the colony's religious legacy. Boston was founded in 1630 by settlers from England, led by John Winthrop. These settlers were from the Puritan tradition, believing that the Church of England—with its hierarchy and ceremonies—needed purifying. As Congregationalists, their church members were directly answerable to God, not a church hierarchy. In 1764, Bostonians were no more eager for an omnipotent political hierarchy than they'd historically been for any overreaching power.

Many people in Boston recognized the dangers of the Sugar Act as soon as word spread about its passage. Sure, any tax imposed by Parliament would have been annoying, but the Sugar Act would impact Massachusetts more than other colonies, so its residents had more reason to be concerned. Despite one member of Parliament, Thomas Whateley, claiming that the Sugar Act "is spread lightly over a great Variety of Subjects, and lies heavy upon none," this simply wasn't true. No other region had as thriving a rum trade as New England, especially Boston, which had over twenty distilleries in the two-mile-long town. For a town already in economic decline, taxing a key import was a big blow. Bostonians needed to make it clear to their elected officials that the Sugar Act—imposed by a governing body three thousand miles away in which they had no representatives—would not be tolerated.[4]

A committee from Boston's town meeting set to work writing instructions to the Massachusetts legislature about the dangers of the Sugar Act. The legislature in Massachusetts, called the General Court, was composed of two houses. The House of Representatives, or Assembly, was the lower house, whose members were popularly elected in their towns by the men eligible to vote, which was the majority of adult men in Massachusetts. The upper house was the Governor's Council, whose members were chosen by the House of Representatives. The General Court sat in session at the Old State House on King Street. These legislators were about to hear an earful.

## BOSTON'S NATIVE SON: SAMUEL ADAMS

One of the committee members petitioning the legislature, Samuel Adams, was not yet on the center stage of politics, although his time in the spotlight would soon come. Adams was a Boston native, heavily influenced by Boston's religion, history and the charter under which Massachusetts was governed. He was born in Boston in 1722 and was provincial Boston to the core. He was a strict Congregationalist, honoring the Sabbath and singing in his church's choir. Religion was at the center of his life—his writings frequently mentioned God's blessings and compared the struggle of colonists to people suffering in the Bible. He also admired his ancestors for bravely settling Massachusetts with no help from their mother country.

Devoted as he was to his heritage and religion, Adams was physically a mess. He was so slovenly that his friends staged an intervention in 1774 to clean him up. They chipped in to buy him a new wardrobe—including a new wig, hat, suit and shoes—so he didn't embarrass himself or Massachusetts in high-wattage political meetings with well-heeled men, especially those from the southern colonies. Adams wasn't particularly handsome, either, with a large head and a squat body. John Singleton Copley did Adams no favors when painting him, as he included both Adams's double chin and large belly. Adams's physical state was made worse because he suffered from what contemporaries called palsy, an affliction that caused him to shake or tremble when he overexerted himself.

Despite being educated at the finest schools—Boston Latin School and then Harvard College—Adams did not have a sharp business mind. After his father died, Samuel was supposed to take over the family's business ventures, but they eventually failed under his (lack of) leadership. His failures continued in the 1750s, when Adams served as a tax collector. He took pity on those who said they couldn't pay their taxes and released them from their financial obligations. This made him popular as a collector but horrible at

John Singleton Copley portrays Samuel Adams in 1770 protesting British policies. Adams intently stares at the viewer while pointing to the charter of Massachusetts. *Museum of Fine Arts, Boston.*

his job. As a young man, he seemed to have a hard time finding a place where he could excel.

The only place where Samuel Adams seemed to be useful was politics, which, in hindsight, was more than enough. He was an intense man wholly committed to his cause and often sounded one note in the late 1760s and

1770s with his frequent complaints about Parliament. He exploited the power of the press by writing fervent newspaper articles criticizing Parliamentary attacks on colonial liberties. Although he rarely drank alcohol, Adams frequented Boston's taverns because he often had something to add to the political conversations taking place there. Opinionated and judgmental, Adams was reviled by many of his contemporaries, and even those who worked alongside him couldn't bear him at times. He was dismissive of people who did not share his political or religious values, frequently criticizing John Hancock for his ostentation and Catholics for their commitment to a pope. The political arena was one place where Adams felt comfortable and exceled, and the Sugar Act was an easy cause for him to rally around.

## Boston Reacts to the Sugar Act

One reason Adams thought so highly of Massachusetts and its history was because the original settlers established their colony with little help or interference from the Crown. The Sugar Act was going to change that—something that Adams and the Boston town committee seized on when they wrote their protest. They argued that the Sugar Act "annihilates our Charter Right to govern & tax ourselves." Worse, it would set a precedent for Parliament to tax the colonies in the future. They wondered if the Sugar Act "may be preparatory to new Taxations upon us." The panic quickly spiraled as they speculated, "For if our Trade may be taxed why not our Lands? Why not the Produce of our Lands & every thing we possess or make use of?" The committee dramatically concluded that if the colonists could not tax themselves but instead had taxes imposed on them by a distant governing power, "Are we not reduced from the Character of free Subjects to the miserable state of tributary Slaves?" It is notable that Boston's town committee members were arguing against the Sugar Act because it violated what they believed to be their rights as British subjects, not a unique or novel sense of liberty.[5]

If a petition to the legislature could not persuade Parliament to repeal the Sugar Act, there were other ways for the colonists to get what they wanted. The colonists had a tradition of violence—a mindset that emigrated with them from England. In the eighteenth century, political leaders understood that people might violently rebel from time to time to protest circumstances they felt were unfair. If colonists believed that their leaders were not doing enough to protect them or their interests, they would rebel. In eighteenth-century Boston, this included riots against brothels, uprisings about food supply and two days of rioting to stop men from being impressed into the Royal Navy. Without a professional police force, towns used the power of the people to impose justice. Magistrates might call out the local militia if extra force was needed. The militia, however, was composed of men within the community, so if most of them sympathized with the rioters—or were the rioters—there was little chance the riots would be stopped. There was a limit to how much people could rebel, though, because if the

A young James Otis Jr., whose cherubic face belies his tormented mind. *The Miriam and Ira D. Wallach Division of Art, Prints and Photographs: Print Collection, New York Public Library.*

government was generally functioning well, mobs were not welcome. But if the Crown pushed through unfavorable laws without colonists' consent, the people had an effective mechanism in place to resist.

A week after the town of Boston issued its instructions to the Massachusetts legislature and before any violence broke out, a political star in Boston, James Otis Jr.—who was more well known than Samuel Adams—further condemned the Sugar Act. James Otis Jr. came from a privileged family in Barnstable, Massachusetts, on Cape Cod. He went to school at Harvard, as did many politically active men at this time, and practiced law after graduating. He was a brilliant lawyer and one John Adams, a young lawyer from Braintree, Massachusetts, and second cousin to Samuel Adams, would later admit to admiring. But Otis was mentally imbalanced. Throughout his life, he would suffer fits—screaming at people for no reason, shattering windows and even firing his gun indoors. His frequent benders didn't help his outbursts. Peter Oliver claimed that Samuel Adams quickly outshone Otis in the political sphere because Adams was "all serpentine Cunning" while Otis was "rash, unguarded, foulmouthed, & openly spitefull." But those inner demons had not fully surfaced yet—in 1764, Otis was still on point.[6]

Otis argued in his pamphlet, *The Rights of British Colonies Asserted and Proved*, that "GEORGE III is the rightful king and sovereign" and that Parliament is the "supreme legislative" body. He believed that the British constitution—which was unwritten—was "the most free one and by far the best now existing on earth." But Otis also claimed that "no parts of His Majesty's dominions can be taxed without their consent." He went further by claiming that the North American colonies should be "represented in some proportion to their number and estates in the grand legislature of the nation." This idea would eventually become the familiar refrain "no taxation without representation." Otis spoke for many in Boston and Massachusetts by proclaiming that even though he had a problem with this tax, he was proud to be a member of the British Empire because of the rights it afforded him. In 1764, the colonists weren't longing to separate from their mother country, just to be heard within it.[7]

Without violent uprisings accompanying Boston's petitions and pamphlets against the Sugar Act, the Crown mostly ignored the bluster of Otis and Boston. This made it easier for those in power to contemplate passing a second tax shortly after the Sugar Act. Colonists began to hear rumors that Grenville wanted to impose a stamp tax on the colonies in 1765. Massachusetts complained to its royal governor, Francis Bernard, saying that only officials elected by the colony should be able to impose taxes within it. Except Governor Bernard wasn't a great person to go to for help. He took over as royal governor of Massachusetts in 1760 after spending a couple of years as governor of New Jersey. Bernard wanted to climb the imperial ladder (and build his personal fortune), and overseeing Massachusetts would help him do that—as would remaining steadfastly loyal to the Crown, even if it upset most of his colony's population. Fortunately for Bernard, a royal governor didn't have to be popular to hold the post. At this time, governors in Massachusetts were appointed by the king. And there was certainly no risk of him being popular. Bernard was often whiny and combative, two traits that Bostonians would come to loathe.

Yet Bernard was the person with the most direct access to the Crown, so townspeople appealed to him first. If colonies needed to pay into the British coffers, Massachusetts claimed to want to raise the money itself. Bernard wrote to the Crown explaining Massachusetts's proposition, but it was a fruitless exercise. Grenville dismissed the request of Bernard and Massachusetts to pass their own tax, for he was determined to push the Stamp Act through Parliament. And because Boston hadn't mounted much of a protest to the Sugar Act, Grenville anticipated a similarly quiet reaction to the Stamp Act. Colonists might complain, but Grenville thought they would eventually get used to paying the taxes. They wouldn't. The Sugar Act would be the last time Boston fought with words alone.

## FROM PAST TO PRESENT

### BOSTON COMMON

*Boston Common (not Commons) is nearly as old as British settlement in Boston. In the seventeenth and eighteenth centuries, it also represented the outskirts of town. The Common was bordered by the Back Bay, a wide bay into which the Charles River flowed before going out into the harbor. When visiting Boston Common today, it is in the same location as it was in the 1760s, but the grounds have changed. It now has more trees and walkways and even tennis courts and a casual restaurant. It lacks the powder house, grazing cows and training militia you would have found in the eighteenth century. Boston Common is the beginning of Boston's red-brick road, the Freedom Trail, so this is the perfect place to begin your journey into the past.*

Boston Common today resembles its eighteenth-century self with plenty of open green space. The Massachusetts State House's golden dome peeks through the trees. *Photograph by the author.*

## BEACON HILL

*If you're on Boston Common, you can see Beacon Hill—it's the northern-facing slope. It's not as much of a hill today as it was in the eighteenth century, when it was three times higher. It was mostly leveled in the 1810s and 1820s. Additionally, you would not have seen the Massachusetts State House dominating the top of the hill. Instead, you would have seen the mansion of Thomas Hancock. Today, Beacon Hill is the highest-rent district in Boston and is the name of both the hill and the neighborhood.*

The leveling of Beacon Hill in the early nineteenth century. The Massachusetts State House is to the right. To the left is a monument commemorating the American Revolution. Both were designed by Charles Bulfinch. *Library of Congress.*

## KING STREET AND LONG WHARF

*King Street was the political, economic and social center of Boston in the eighteenth century. For all of its action, it wasn't a very long street unless you factored in Long Wharf. The eighteenth-century shoreline would have been near Kilby Street today, but now it extends another half mile. This land was filled in during the first half of the nineteenth century. King Street was renamed State Street after Bostonians rejected the king's rule, and that is the name it bears today.*

*At the end of State Street, you'll still find Long Wharf—it ends in the same location today as it did in the eighteenth century—but because* of the landfill, it no longer earns the name Long Wharf. It is a functioning wharf with boats traveling to Charlestown and the Boston Harbor islands. One building from the Revolutionary era remains on Long Wharf. It was owned by John Hancock in the 1760s and today houses the Chart House restaurant.

*Left*: King Street ran from this intersection down to Long Wharf. The Old State House is visible in the right foreground. *Photograph by author.*

*Below*: Long Wharf today includes a hotel, restaurant and the New England Aquarium. *Photograph by the author.*

# 2

# WORDS MAY NOT HURT, BUT STICKS AND STONES DO

*Key Player: Thomas Hutchinson, Culprit and Victim*

Parliament had unintentionally endangered one of Massachusetts's most loyal subjects. Andrew Oliver came from a prominent Boston family and was a loyal servant of the British Crown. And he was now in harm's way. Oliver had been appointed to collect the latest Parliamentary tax, the Stamp Act, passed in March 1765. Unlike the nonviolent reactions to the Sugar Act, Bostonians were so opposed to this tax that a local mob planned to target those who intended to enforce it. Oliver would be the first victim caught in the mob's crosshairs. Boston's rebels were about to show that their ideological protests of the Sugar Act were a thing of the past.

George Grenville, prime minister of Great Britain, was adamant that the colonists help to pay the heavy expense of administering the North American colonies and decrease the debt caused by the French and Indian War. The Sugar Act alone wouldn't solve the problem, so the Stamp Act was Grenville's next solution. It decreed that any printed documents now needed a stamp, which resembled a notary more than a postage stamp. Newspapers, deeds, diplomas, marriage licenses, playing cards, almanacs and liquor licenses all needed these new stamps. Adding to Bostonians' annoyance, various items were taxed differently, with over forty tax rates. For example, appointments to public office were subjected to the highest tax, and items written in any language other than English were taxed double the standard rate. Bostonians heard about the Stamp Act in May 1765, and it was to take effect on November 1, 1765. This six-month lead gave them time to prepare an adequate response before the stamps could be distributed.

Boston's rebels first reacted to the Stamp Act in much the same way as they had the Sugar Act: by claiming that it violated their rights under the British Constitution. In September 1765, a Boston town committee wrote a petition that claimed "the most essential Rights of British Subjects are those of being represented in the same Body which exercises the Power of levying Taxes upon them." It wasn't just that rebel leaders didn't want to pay the tax. (Although that was surely part of it.) They believed that being taxed by a governing body—in which they were not represented—violated their rights as British subjects. Boston's petition outlined another legitimate fear: Bostonians consenting to this tax would "afford a Precedent for the Parliament to tax us, in all future Time, & in all such Ways & Measures." If they paid this tax now, they questioned whether the British Empire would ever stop taxing them.[8]

The Stamp Act was loathsome to more than just the Boston town committee because, unlike the Sugar Act, it affected all people. Few would be able to escape paying for the stamps, although the tax disproportionately affected the most vocal people in society, including lawyers, merchants and newspaper writers. This ensured an outcry from many of those who were the mouthpieces to the rest of Boston and Massachusetts. Newspaper editorialists criticized it, lawyers argued that it wasn't constitutional and ministers condemned it during their sermons. The responses in Boston against the Stamp Act were so intense that Massachusetts lieutenant governor Thomas Hutchinson feared the Stamp Act might lead to violence. "I hope we shall be able to keep peace in the execution of the stamp act notwithstanding all the newspaper threats," he wrote to a contact in London in August 1765. Hutchinson's concern was valid, as he'd previously experienced how vindictive Bostonians could be.[9]

# BOSTON VERSUS THOMAS HUTCHINSON

Many people in Boston had mistrusted Hutchinson for years, mostly for what they considered to be his shady, inbred politics. One issue Bostonians had with Hutchinson revolved around the constitutionality of writs of assistance. A writ of assistance is similar to a search warrant, and in 1761, Parliament made it legal for customs officials to file for writs of assistance. Once a writ was granted, any building—including private homes—and ships could then be searched for smuggled goods. This would grant customs officials (already a detestable lot) a frightening amount of power when trying to find smugglers, which characterized many merchants in Boston. Knowing the potential danger of writs, James Otis Jr. fought against them in court, arguing that they violated British constitutional rights. Otis was arguing as a British subject, claiming that the writs violated the rights he felt he was afforded as such. Otis lost this case in court, and the judge who upheld the decision was none other than Thomas Hutchinson.

Hutchinson was no stranger to James Otis Jr. in Boston's political scene. Otis had previously targeted Hutchinson when Governor Bernard named Hutchinson chief justice of Massachusetts in 1760. Otis was annoyed by this appointment for three reasons: first, Hutchinson got the job over Otis's own father; second, Hutchinson already held several political posts in Massachusetts, which seemed corrupt and a conflict of interest; and finally, Hutchinson, the new chief justice of the Supreme Court, had no legal experience. Surely someone without a firm grasp on the law would not be able to protect Massachusetts law effectively. Peter Oliver claimed that after Hutchinson's appointment, both Otis Senior and Junior "exerted themselves…to revenge their Disappointment, in Mr. Hutchinson's Destruction." When Hutchinson supported the writs of assistance decision shortly after taking over as chief justice, it pushed Otis over the edge. Otis railed against Hutchinson in the newspapers, establishing a years-long personal vendetta between the two men.[10]

Even as a staunch Loyalist, Hutchinson was as much of an American as James Otis Jr. or Samuel Adams. He was born in the colonies, after all, with deep roots in Massachusetts. His great-great-grandmother was Anne Hutchinson, who was banished from Massachusetts by Governor John Winthrop for her radical religious ideas. Hutchinson was fascinated by his heritage and quite proud of it—so much so that he began writing a two-volume history of the colony of Massachusetts. Why shouldn't he have been proud? The Hutchinsons had achieved great success in America. His family had been merchants for successive generations, amassing a fortune that afforded Hutchinson eight homes, two wharves and several shops.

Hutchinson was an easy target because of his wealth, multiple political offices and loyalty to the Crown, but—and this few credited him with—he was also a family man. He was a devoted husband who didn't marry again after his first love and wife, Peggy, died during childbirth in 1754. Her death devastated him. He remained close to his five children throughout their lives, especially doting on his youngest daughter, Peggy, named for the woman whose life had been taken giving birth to her. Hutchinson was

A thirty-year-old Thomas Hutchinson in his only known portrait. It was painted in 1741 by Edward Truman, over twenty years before Hutchinson was at the center of Boston's political drama. *Collection of the Massachusetts Historical Society.*

inconsolable when Peggy became sick in her early twenties—her illness and care became his purpose. Peggy died at just twenty-three years old, and Hutchinson's grief was all-consuming. In his tumultuous and eventful life, watching his beloved wife and daughter die were the worst things to happen to him—tragedies from which he never quite recovered. Although his actions frequently belied this, he was an emotionally sensitive man. In the late 1760s, he suffered a nervous breakdown that kept him confined to his home for several weeks.

The vitriol Hutchinson inspired among colonists seemed disproportionate to his actual political beliefs, but he lacked the charisma and goodwill to repair relationships with his fellow colonists. He refused to adapt to the shifting politics in North America, believing that politics should proceed as they had for decades (with him and his family benefiting from such a system). Privately, Hutchinson opposed the passage of the Stamp Act, thinking it "would be bad both to the nation & the colonies." But as a man in service of Great Britain, he conceded that Parliament had the authority to pass the Stamp Act, and the colonists should therefore comply with it. So while he didn't believe in the new tax, he went along with it, as did Governor Bernard.[11]

## TAKING TO THE STREETS

As Hutchinson and Bernard were falling in lockstep to comply with the Stamp Act, a group of men organized to oppose it. The Loyal Nine was a social club in Boston consisting of (no big surprise) nine men in their twenties and thirties, mostly artisans and shopkeepers. This group would eventually evolve and expand later in the year to become the Sons of Liberty, which was filled with names more recognizable to us today: Samuel Adams, Paul Revere, John Hancock and John Adams. (A relative of Hutchinson referred to them as the "Sons of Anarchy," so the term "liberty" was open to interpretation.)[12]

The Loyal Nine's first target was Stamp Act collector Andrew Oliver. Oliver and Hutchinson were brothers-in-law, as their families frequently intermarried—solidifying both families' political and economic stature and incurring the resentment of Bostonians. Oliver came from a long line of merchants who had been in North America for nearly as long as its settlement by the Puritans. Being the Stamp Act collector of Massachusetts was a potentially lucrative position, which is why someone of Oliver's standing received it. What Oliver couldn't have known when accepting the post was the violence he and the other collectors would be subjected to. Samuel Adams claimed that after the riots broke out, "every Stampman trembled." Oliver was in danger.[13]

The Loyal Nine enlisted the help of two local, rival street gangs—one from the North End and one from the South End—to intimidate British officials. To fully realize who these men were, know that they got together annually on Pope's Day, November 5, and participated in an enormous street brawl. The fight occurred under the guise of capturing the other side's pope, a figure made from papier-mâché, but the point was to rumble. Bones were broken in the process and gashes earned; even a small child was accidentally killed during the 1764 Pope's Day fight. This fracas always happened downtown, in plain view of nonparticipating townspeople, demonstrating a tradition of street violence. The leader of the South End gang, Ebenezer Mackintosh, recruited these tough and aggressive fighters, who included rope workers and longshoremen, to work together, instead of as separate gangs, to resist the Stamp Act.

With the mob now in place, Boston became the first town in the North American colonies to rebel violently against the Stamp Act. Because orchestrated violence was an established part of Boston's political and cultural landscape, mobs opposing an unjust tax were unlikely to face much resistance on the streets. The mob not only sought to embarrass Oliver but also to make it difficult and undesirable for him or anybody else to enforce the Stamp Act. On August 14, a mob hanged Oliver in effigy from a massive elm tree at the edge of town, visible on the main road in and out of Boston. This tree would later be known as the Liberty Tree. People coming into Boston even stopped to have Oliver's effigy mockingly stamp their goods. In the evening, the mob paraded through Boston and, as Governor Bernard noted, passed by "the Town House, bringing the Effigy with them, and knowing we were sitting in Council Chamber, they gave three Huzzas by way of defiance, and passed on." The horde then headed down to Oliver's dock and destroyed his recently erected office. Rumor had it that the stamps would be held there once delivered, so the participants preemptively made such storage an impossibility. Hutchinson claimed that "in a few minutes the building was level with the ground." The mob was just getting warmed up.[14]

Oliver's house was next. He was urged by neighbors and loved ones, including Hutchinson, to leave his house. Hutchinson had arrived during the action and even attempted crowd control by demanding that the men disperse—a brave act in defense of his family. Punishing Hutchinson for his boldness, the crowd threw rocks at him. It then turned its attention back to Oliver's home and broke his windows and burned his coach. Nearly two thousand people watched the parade and bonfire, turning this from an isolated event committed by a local mob into a concerted action by the public. Rebels justified such violence by claiming that their attempts to peacefully

John Singleton Copley's portrait of Andrew Oliver, completed in the early 1760s. Oliver's grave countenance here likely matched his reaction after mobs targeted him. *National Portrait Gallery, Smithsonian Institution.*

protest the Stamp Act with petitions had not been effective. Satisfied with their show of force, the mob demanded that Oliver publicly resign at the Liberty Tree.

Oliver capitulated the very next day. In resigning, he reinforced violence as an acceptable way for rebels to address their grievances. Samuel Adams gloated after the destruction of Oliver's effigy, house and stamp office. Boston, he claimed, made the Oliver riots "a Day which ought to be for ever remembered in America." When Oliver resigned from his post in Boston, he set in motion other emboldened mobs in frustrated cities to similarly harass and intimidate their Stamp Act collectors. General Thomas Gage claimed that the "populace of Boston took the Lead in the Riots," but shortly after, mobs terrorized authorities in Rhode Island, whose Stamp Act collector then abandoned his post. Crowds further intimidated officials believed to be connected to the Stamp Act in New York, Pennsylvania, Maryland and North and South Carolina. After word spread about such activity, sometimes just the threat of violence would prompt Stamp Act collectors from other colonies to resign. With Stamp Act collectors abandoning their jobs throughout North America, other men had no desire to accept the now widely available posts as Stamp Act collectors.[15]

## MOB MENTALITY

While Stamp Act resistance was spreading like smallpox across North America, eager rebels in Boston didn't waste time targeting their next victim. Twelve days after terrorizing Andrew Oliver, a different mob was on the prowl. These were mostly lower-class workers, while Oliver's mob had comprised all levels of Boston's society. The crowd first went to the homes of two British customs officials and did some damage. With their destructive appetites whetted, mob members then went to the home of their old friend Thomas Hutchinson in the North End. Hutchinson had a fine, three-story, brick mansion that had been built nearly a century ago and was where he was born fifty-four years earlier. Fortunately, Hutchinson got word that the mob was coming and ordered his family to flee. His daughter, Sally, was justifiably afraid for her father and insisted that she would not leave the house without him. As a father, he was likely terrified that his child was minutes away from being in the face of an uncontrollable mob. Out of fear for his daughter's safety, but not his own—he had already shown he was stubborn enough to try to stare down a mob—Hutchinson fled to a neighbor's house, and just in time. The horde descended on his mansion, aiming to lay waste.

Under the enhanced protection and anonymity of darkness, the mob spent hours destroying Hutchinson's home. They broke all of his windows. Shattered his furniture. Stole his paintings and money. Thugs took manuscripts from his office—many of them valuable originals, collected for his history of Massachusetts—and flung them out into the street. Vindictively, the mob chopped down the trees in his garden. Leveled his fence. Not surprisingly, they drank all of the alcohol stored in his cellar. (These spirits undoubtedly led to more spirited violence.) Neighbors must have been frightened as they heard wood splintering, glass breaking and men shouting.

The smell of the mob would have permeated the North End that night—a blend of smoke, wine, sweat and hate. The men stopped only at daybreak, when they were trying to rip down the cupola from Hutchinson's house. They were likely too exhausted to continue, especially in the midst of August—typically humid in Boston—for it was an hours-long project they had embarked on. And if such a thing can be measured, it was a success. By morning, what remained was the shell of a house and a damaged roof. Hutchinson was stunned by how thorough the mob had been and estimated that nearly ten thousand people came by in the passing days to gawk at what was left of his home and possessions.

Hutchinson was so destitute after the attacks that he showed up for work in court the next day in the clothes that he had been wearing the day before. What a sight for onlookers to see this noble man knocked down a peg or two. Hutchinson knew that the court couldn't operate without him, so he arrived, apologized for his appearance and reminded the men sitting in court that he had never supported the Stamp Act. Hutchinson claimed, "[I] did all

Lieutenant Governor Thomas Hutchinson's mansion in the North End. *Courtesy of the American Antiquarian Society.*

in my Power, & strove as much as in me lay, to prevent it." It takes pride, courage and foolhardiness to pretend to go about with business as usual after such an attack. It may have also been a desperate attempt to earn people's sympathy. Or he may have been searching for some shred of normalcy after a devastating attack on his personal property, and fulfilling royal duties could have provided that.[16]

In the days after the riot at his house, Hutchinson spent a lot of time writing to what he hoped would be sympathetic friends and colleagues in London. Hutchinson called the attack the "most barbarous outrage" and an act full of "hellish rage" perpetuated by a "hellish crew." He declared that such destruction had "never been seen in America." His letters were almost formulaic, with only details varying. Hutchinson would describe the attack, offer an inventory of what had been destroyed and warn how dangerous it was to have uncontrollable mobs loose in the streets. To one correspondent, he wrote, "Axes split down the door," most beds were "cut open & feathers thrown out of the windows" and his "garden fence was laid flat." Hutchinson told one colleague that he had been able to pick up some pieces of his clothing lying throughout town the next day, but it was mostly a hopeless endeavor, as the majority of his possessions were completely ruined. It would have been an embarrassing scavenger hunt.[17]

In addition to compassion, Hutchinson sought justice and repayment for the destruction. He hardly received it. No one was ever punished for the riot, largely because no one was willing to name the perpetrators. One of the leaders of the Oliver riot, Ebenezer Mackintosh, was arrested for his supposed involvement in the Hutchinson riot. He was later released, though, after threats were made that the customs house would be destroyed next if Mackintosh remained in custody. Even if townspeople had identified other members of the mob, no man would have been brave enough to step forward and prosecute them, as it would have meant assured destruction of his own property. Governor Bernard wrote to London, "In short, the Town of Boston is in the possession of an incensed and implacable Mob; I have no force to oppose…them." No one would ultimately be punished for the damage caused, but Hutchinson continued to lobby for payment.[18]

In a painfully detailed petition dated October 25, 1765, Hutchinson actually pleaded with the king for compensation. For eight pages, Hutchinson reported to King George III what had been "destroyed or carried away" from his house and the value of each item. He listed gilt frames, mahogany tables, china dishes, a walnut table and chairs, a "large looking glass" and feather beds. One can imagine the awe, and likely the jealous anger, of the men who saw such luxury during the destruction. These were items that they would never be able to afford, and worse, a man they despised possessed them. Hutchinson's list also included possessions that belonged to his maid, housekeeper and coachmen, further highlighting his elite status. Hutchinson estimated that all of the destroyed items totaled £2,200 sterling, a

The innocuous-looking King George III, who took over the throne in 1760 when he was just twenty-two years old. *The Miriam and Ira D. Wallach Division of Art, Prints and Photographs: Print Collection, New York Public Library.*

considerable sum. That amount would be more than a craftsman—with annual earnings of less than £60—could expect to earn in his lifetime. In the end, the Massachusetts House of Representatives compensated Hutchinson for his house, but in agreeing to their sum of money, which was not enough to pay for all of the items stolen or destroyed, Hutchinson also had to agree to exonerate the unnamed rioters.[19]

So Hutchinson wasn't adequately compensated, no one was punished and, worst of all, the riot had been committed by a rogue mob. The mob that destroyed Hutchinson's home wasn't one sanctioned by the Loyal Nine or other rebel leaders. These men largely rioted as an outlet for their own grievances, not necessarily to protest against the Stamp Act. Both Loyalists and rebels agreed that these men were dangerous. Hutchinson acknowledged that the "encouragers of the first mob never intended matters should go [to] this length" and that only bad things can come when such dangerous people "are let loose in a government where there is not constant authority at hand." Even Samuel Adams knew that mobs couldn't act on their own or life would be chaotic. While he was gleeful about the mob that destroyed Oliver's home, he called the mob that targeted Hutchinson "truly *mobbish*" and claimed that "the cause of this riot is not known publickly." To keep the rebels respectable, future actions would have to be more organized.[20]

# A NONVIOLENT SOLUTION

Violence wasn't always necessary to send a message to Parliament, especially if the North American colonies could work together to oppose the Stamp Act. In an unprecedented act of solidarity, several colonies got together in October 1765 to discuss how to deal with the Stamp Act. For two weeks, the twenty-seven delegates of the Stamp Act Congress, as it was known, discussed Parliamentary power and how far it could extend. The congress passed a series of resolutions, including "no taxes can be imposed on [Englishmen] but with their own consent, given personally or by their representatives." This the colonists had said before. No taxation without representation had become a familiar refrain, one that the Boston town committee had claimed months earlier. Now, however, the colonies were saying it together. But still, these were just ideas.[21]

Where the Stamp Act Congress was most effective was in imposing a boycott of British goods. After weeks of violence in Boston and throughout the colonies, resistance to the Stamp Act had morphed into a nonviolent but highly effective financial punishment. This boycott was especially unnerving for British merchants who had extended credit to American merchants and were justifiably concerned that these debts wouldn't be paid back. These merchants lobbied Parliament to repeal the Stamp Act, citing the longstanding and beneficial trade between the colonies and mother country that would end if the boycott continued. Having British subjects in Great Britain oppose the Stamp Act made it more difficult for Parliament to continue justifying the tax.

Despite the challenges to the Stamp Act at home and abroad, no one knew what might happen on the day the act was supposed to go into effect. Would the stamps be distributed? Could they be distributed? Governor Bernard expected trouble and ordered the militia to protect Boston. (Bernard was only brave from a distance. In mid-August, he had fled Boston to be out of the mob's grasp.) Not surprisingly, the militia refused to turn out. When November 1 arrived, Boston was melodramatic about the day, treating it as if it were a day of mourning, with actions typical of such an occasion: flags at half-mast, businesses shuttered, bells tolling. Where a stamp should have appeared in a newspaper instead appeared a skull with crossbones. That afternoon at the Liberty Tree, a crowd hung and then cut down the effigies of British officials, which they then "tore to pieces," according to Bernard.[22]

After a brief period of uncertainty, business went on as usual in Boston without the stamps. And without British goods. No stamps were ever distributed in Massachusetts. Abroad, British merchants were growing warier of the Stamp Act as each day went by without their goods selling and North American debts languishing on the books.

A placeholder for where a stamp would have appeared. It reads, "This is the Place to affix the STAMP." *Library of Congress.*

They put more pressure on Parliament. And so, less than a year after the Stamp Act passed and before any revenue had been collected, Parliament was sufficiently compelled to repeal the tax in March 1766. It would be a decision that King George III would come to regret.

Boston was jubilant when the repeal was announced in May. May 19 was designated as a day of celebration, and what a day it was. The Beacon Hill mansion of John Hancock was designated the party spot. Hancock paid for a fireworks display over Boston Common and brought out more than one hundred gallons of wine for people to imbibe and rejoice. The Liberty Tree, which months earlier had been the site of effigies and intimidation, was now decorated with festive streamers. Cannons were fired; drums were beating. Music filled the spring air. As they had demonstrated the previous August, Bostonians knew how to riot against injustice. But they equally, if not better, knew how to celebrate when their message was heard loud and clear. The party continued the next day, as John Hancock hosted over two dozen merchants at the Bunch of Grapes tavern on King Street. Samuel Adams believed the Stamp Act was repealed because the colonies had stuck together, but Boston partied as if the victory was its own.[23]

## "SAVING OF APPEARANCES"

The decision to repeal was, without equivocation, a mistake by Parliament because it demonstrated that violence and a willful neglect of British policies were now tolerated. Parliament attempted to mitigate its appeasement. But George Grenville, the man who presided over Parliament during the passage of the Stamp Act, was no longer running the show. King George III had replaced him with the Marquis of Rockingham, who was left the unenviable task of cleaning up a mess that he had not created. Rockingham knew he needed a creative solution to reassert the power of the British Empire, so he looked to history for inspiration. In 1720, Parliament had passed a Declaratory Act for Ireland that stated that Parliament could pass laws for Ireland at any time. The people of Ireland would still be allowed to legislate themselves and have their own faiths, but the Crown was their ultimate authority. When the act was passed, Ireland broke out in small rebellions but eventually fell in line and became subject to the Declaratory Act. Not understanding the spatial difference between Ireland and the colonies, Rockingham believed the same type of law could solve Parliament's problem in North America.

On the same day Parliament repealed the Stamp Act, it passed the Declaratory Act, which stated that Parliament had the right to tax the colonists at any time. It claimed that the North American colonies "ought to be, subordinate unto, and dependent" on Great Britain and that Parliament had the "full power and authority" to make whatever laws it wanted "in all cases whatsoever." But Parliament had just proven that wasn't true. Peter Oliver, ever a biting commentator, said of the Declaratory Act, "This might be Termed, saving of Appearances." That is exactly what it seemed to the colonists as well, because the Stamp Act had been passed, condemned, ignored, boycotted and then repealed, proving to rebels that Parliament did not, in fact, have authority over them in all cases.[24]

Hutchinson believed the Declaratory Act was flawed. He bluntly stated to a colleague in London, "You have passed an act declaring us subject…A bare declaration that we are subject…does not, in fact, make us so." He was right about that. The Declaratory Act could be easily enforced from a close distance in Ireland, but the same could not be said for the colonies. Hutchinson explained, "Ireland is under your constant inspection," and so "every act of disobedience is known immediately," which allowed Britain to easily squash any rebellion. This was not true for the colonies. It took six weeks for news to travel from Boston to London. "The colonies are too remote," Hutchinson foretold, and if Britain wanted colonial submission, "something further is therefore necessary in order to secure their obedience."[25]

This perceptive observation about the colonies and their (lack of) obedience demonstrated that Hutchinson had, at times, a greater understanding of and sympathy toward the colonies than contemporaries gave him credit for. A few months after asserting that the Declaratory Act was not tenable, Hutchinson again predicted the future. He wrote to a contact in London that colonists may have proclaimed their loyalty to the Empire after the Stamp Act repeal, but "I fear the present calm after so violent a storm will be but of short continuance." It was prophetic. Parliament would soon try to tax the colonists again to demonstrate its authority over them. And Boston rebels would again remind the Crown that they would not allow themselves to be subjected by a distant power. Indeed, a more violent storm was coming.[26]

## FROM PAST TO PRESENT

### LIBERTY TREE

*The Liberty Tree was an elm tree on the road into Boston, and it sat near the Neck at the edge of town. If it were still around today, it would be on busy Washington Street in Chinatown, with Essex as the cross street. There is a plaque commemorating the tree on the second story of the brick building that houses the MBTA Chinatown Orange Line* stop. Your best imagination will be necessary here to picture the tree in the eighteenth century. Wipe away the tall buildings, subway and people but not necessarily the traffic. Although you wouldn't have seen cars in Boston in the colonial period, this part of town was the main route in and out of Boston, so you would have seen men on horses, with or without carts, coming in and going out. In the 1760s, you would have also likely seen an effigy or two hanging in the tree as you passed by.

Finding the Liberty Tree isn't easy on this busy corner. Above the subway entrance (marked with a *T*) is a bas-relief plaque commemorating its site. *Photograph by the author.*

## OLD STATE HOUSE

*This is one of the most majestic buildings in all of Boston and sits along the Freedom Trail. Built in 1713, it was the seat of government power until the gold-domed Massachusetts State House took its place in 1798. Buying a ticket to the museum affords you the opportunity to imagine a view of Boston's seafaring commerce in the 1700s. Head up to the second floor and go into the room facing east. There are three large windows, but the one in the center is the best to gaze out of. Look down at King Street—today it is State Street—and picture a bustling port with tall-masted ships, lots of shops and many people and horse-drawn carts milling about. Finally, envision yourself as royal governor, watching a mob parade in front of you while carrying an effigy of one of your appointed officials.*

The dignified three-story Old State House sits among the sleek architecture of the more recent past. *Photograph by the author.*

## THOMAS HUTCHINSON'S HOUSE

*Thomas Hutchinson's house was rebuilt after its destruction in 1765 but later demolished in 1833. Today, you can visit the site of his house in Boston's North End. There is a plaque on Garden Court Street, a quiet, narrow street, just up the road from Paul Revere's house, although Revere was not a neighbor of Hutchinson's when his house was destroyed. When coming up the street from North Square, the plaque will be on the left side of the building. It is heavily oxidized and green. The plaque was erected by the City of Boston in 1930, ironically without any mention of what makes his residence so famous. (This was likely a conscious decision not to commemorate a mob that attacked the private home of a government official.) Do your best to picture the grand, three-story, brick mansion in this spot and then imagine the terror you would feel seeing a mob coming toward you, intent on destruction.*

This neglected and unremarkable plaque shows the location of Hutchinson's mansion on Garden Court Street. *Photograph by the author.*

# 3

# THE CONSEQUENCES
# OF TORCHING LIBERTY

## *Key Player: The Rising Star of John Hancock*

The king was furious with Massachusetts—again—and with good reason. The rebel leaders in Boston seemed to take pleasure in defying the Crown. But now they had taken it too far. Boston opposing acts of Parliament was one thing—even though the Declaratory Act firmly stated Parliament's authority over the colonies—but just a year and a half later, men in Boston were not only questioning Parliament's authority but also persuading other colonies to join their defiance. Crown officials realized the dangers if other colonies fell in with what Peter Oliver termed the "Massachusetts Standard." It would not do. Boston's latest rebellious tract would need to be erased from North America's consciousness.[27]

Bostonians would argue that their protest was justified. In 1767, Parliament had passed a new round of taxes. The Townshend Duties—named after Charles Townshend, the member of Parliament who proposed the plan—required colonists to pay taxes on imported British goods, including tea, glass, paper and clothing. These duties were passed for the same reasons that the Sugar and Stamp Acts were: to pay for the cost of running the North American empire. The stated goals of the Townshend Duties included "defraying the charge of the administration of justice, and the support of civil government" and "further defraying the expenses of defending, protecting, and securing, the said dominions." Parliament was determined to have the colonists pay taxes in some form, especially after the regretfully repealed Stamp Act a year earlier.[28]

Massachusetts wasted little time opposing the Townshend Duties, with the House of Representatives petitioning the king for their repeal. James Otis Jr., Samuel Adams and John Hancock helped draft the petition. Dated January 20, 1768, it claimed that the colonists could no longer be considered free if Parliament continued to take their property—in this case, money—without representing them in the government. "Your People must then regret their unhappy fate in having only the name left of free Subjects," they complained. The House of Representatives also asked their agent in London, "Is there any real difference between this act and the stamp act?" Surely not, as both attempted to raise revenue and both were passed without the consent of those being taxed. The House accused the Townshend Duties of being "burthensome to trade, ruinous to the nation."[29]

Charles Townshend, whose eponymous taxes prompted outrage among rebels. *The Miriam and Ira D. Wallach Division of Art, Prints and Photographs: Print Collection, New York Public Library.*

The Massachusetts House of Representatives also sent a letter to other North American colonies asking them to join Massachusetts by boycotting British goods, which would render the Townshend Duties moot. This was the letter that upset the Crown. Drafted by Samuel Adams in January 1768, the letter reminded the other colonies that taxation without representation was unconstitutional. Adams argued that the Townshend Duties, "with the sole & express purpose of raising a Revenue, are Infringements of [the colonists'] natural and constitutional rights." Because colonists were not represented in Parliament and because the duties "grant their Property without their consent," they couldn't possibly be synonymous with the rights of British subjects. The circular letter, as it became known, requested that the nonimportation agreement be in effect until the Townshend Duties were repealed.[30]

This attempt by Massachusetts to galvanize the North American colonies against British policy didn't go over well with King George III and Governor Bernard, both of whom demanded that the circular letter be retracted. Lord Hillsborough, the newly elected secretary of state to the colonies, speaking on behalf of His Majesty, asked the House of Representatives to "immediately...exert your utmost influence to defeat this flagatious attempt to disturb the Public Peace." Frustration and loathing ooze through his letter. In a nod to due process, the House decided the matter of rescinding the letter should be put to a vote. Voting on the issue showed an attempt to operate within the confines of the British government, and Bernard hoped his assembly wouldn't let him down. (He would be disappointed.)[31]

In June 1768, the House of Representatives voted. It was voting on whether to retract the circular letter, but on a deeper level, it was also casting yeas and nays to determine if Crown officials could tell it what it could and could not do. In an overwhelming majority of 92 to 17, the legislature unsurprisingly refused to bow to the pressure of the British and voted not to recall the circular letter. The "Glorious 92"—the lofty name given to the men who would not rescind the letter—were heralded in print and silver, with Paul Revere creating a punchbowl honoring the men and moment. To many in Boston, the Glorious 92 were men who represented firm principles, even in the face of political pressure and tyranny.

With its decision in hand, the House of Representatives wrote to Bernard outlining why it voted not to rescind. Its letter is an absolutely masterful piece of politics. It explained their political position, argued for the importance of protecting their rights as British subjects and insulted the governor—everything necessary after such a controversial decision. The House had practical reasons not to rescind it, the legislators reasoned. "The circular letters have been sent, and many of them have been answered; those answers are now in the public papers," they argued. The House did not see any reason to retract the letter now since the ideas in the circular letter were already circulating in North America. It also claimed that it was a "native, inherent, and indefeasible right" of British subjects to "petition the King for the redress of grievances," provided that they do so in a dutiful way "without tumult, disorder, or confusion." (That bit about protesting without tumult or disorder is pretty silly considering the way Boston's rebels had reacted to the Stamp Act two years earlier.) But their letter claimed that they were committed to their decision not to rescind, as they have been guided by "a clear and determined sense of duty to God, to our King, our country, and our latest posterity." Here comes the coup de grace: the House then attacked Bernard and "humbly pray[s]" that in the future, Bernard "may be influenced by the same principles" as those of the Massachusetts legislature.

Bostonians weren't just defiant; they also celebrated, idealized and justified such brazenness and taunted their leaders while doing so.[32]

Governor Bernard was furious at this slap in the face and dissolved the House of Representatives as punishment. He was clearly exasperated. Not only did his own legislature not support him, they seemed to be actively conspiring against him. And don't get Bernard started on what was happening among the masses. In March 1768, shortly after the circular letter had been distributed, Bernard wrote to Lord Hillsborough telling him of the chaos on the streets of Boston, referring to the annual celebration of the Stamp Act repeal. Since 1766, Bostonians had annually and raucously celebrated the repeal of the Stamp Act. Bernard wrote, "A great Number of People together of all Kinds, Sexes, and Ages, many of them shewed a great Disposition to the utmost disorder." He weakly claimed that their "Yells and outcries were quite terrible." Bernard warned Hillsborough—as he frequently did—that he could not prevent Boston's mobs or their violence.[33]

## John Hancock Takes on Customs Officials

The Crown had learned (a tiny bit) from the Stamp Act debacle and knew that it would need help to enforce the Townshend Duties; consequently, Parliament headquartered new customs officials in Boston. The men sent to enforce the duties were loathsome, earnestly patrolling the harbors, eager to stop and search nearly any vessel. Many people in Boston resented that the Crown thrust new royal officials upon them, whom rebels saw as examples of arbitrary power with no affiliation to the colony they were supposed to regulate. But despite their new strength in numbers, customs officers still found it difficult to enforce the regulations in Boston. They were frequently harassed by townspeople, especially in the summer of 1768, as rebels sought to defend the honor of one of the richest and most popular men in town: John Hancock.

While Hancock is most famous for being the first (and largest) signatory of the Declaration of Independence, his penmanship wasn't what made Bostonians love him. When we first meet him here in 1768, he is thirty-one years of age and already the wealthiest man in Boston. John Hancock came into his money through an inheritance, but his circumstances were not those of a child born into a wealthy family. John's father died when John was just eight years old, and John's mother's financial circumstances—never overly comfortable to begin with—quickly deteriorated. John's uncle, Thomas, and his wife, Lydia, were childless and asked John's mother if they could adopt her eldest son and raise him as their own, where he would live a life of privilege. Thomas was a self-made man who had created a massive shipping house in Boston, the House of Hancock. John's mother consented, and young John literally moved on up to his uncle's house on the top of Beacon Hill. John would attend the most prestigious schools—Boston Latin and Harvard College—and then work for his uncle's business until Thomas passed away. His widow retained some of the Hancock estate, but the majority of it went to John. On the day of his uncle's death, John became the wealthiest man in Boston, head of the House of Hancock and one of the largest employers in Massachusetts.

Conspicuous consumption was a trademark of Hancock's. He liked to look rich, so he imported the finest fashions from London and paraded around Boston with gilded buttons, large wigs and embroidered jackets, all carried regally on his lithe frame. John Singleton Copley's portrait of Hancock shows his delicate facial features and demonstrates his love of fashion. When Hancock was named captain of an honorary militia in Boston, he hired his tailor in London to design an elaborate and sumptuous new uniform for his position. Satisfied with the sartorial upgrade, he then purchased similar uniforms for every man in the militia. Hancock even rode around Boston in a gold carriage, at a time when having any carriage was a sign of sizeable wealth. Hancock wanted to remain singular among men.

Hancock's money also bought admiration—something that was important to him. He was quite generous to Bostonians: donating Bibles or pews to needy churches; installing walkways on Boston Common so people weren't traipsing through the mud or dust, depending on the season; and giving wood to the poor so they could keep warm in the winter. He also funded the entire re-construction of the church he attended, Brattle Street Church. His popularity led Hancock to frequently win appointments to local elections. He was consistently the top vote-getter for the Massachusetts General Court and town councils. In 1769, for example, he received 500 votes out of a possible 508 votes for the Massachusetts House of Representatives.

Hancock's popularity came in handy when the new customs officials stationed in Boston targeted him and his business. As a merchant, the Townshend Duties could severely cripple the House of Hancock's profits. Like any good rebel, Hancock wasn't afraid to skirt the law. Hancock was a frequent smuggler, as most merchants were at this time, and he didn't want any customs officials snooping into his business—Townshend Duties or not.

John Singleton Copley painted John Hancock in 1765. Hancock sits overlooking a ledger book, in control of the House of Hancock. Satisfy his ego and glance an extra minute longer. *Museum of Fine Arts, Boston.*

In April 1768, one of Hancock's ships, *Lydia*, landed in Boston. As would be routine, two customs agents went to inspect the cargo, but Hancock dismissed them. With his oversized ego and keen business interests, waving a British official away would have likely come easily to Hancock. Later that night, one of the customs officials, Owen Richards, snuck onto Hancock's ship to see the goods he was sure Hancock was hiding. While he was snooping on board *Lydia*, Hancock and several of his employees caught the customs official red-handed.

Hancock and his lackeys demanded to see Richards's search warrant. When he wasn't able to produce one, Hancock's men grabbed him and dangled him over the side of the ship, threatening to drop him into the harbor until he admitted that he had no business being on the ship. A humiliated Richards conceded and was released. He did, in fact, have no business being on the ship at that hour. It wasn't Richards's property, he wasn't there in an official capacity and he certainly hadn't been given permission to board Hancock's ship. But this episode set a dangerous precedent for how Bostonians could treat customs officials. While the episode heightened Hancock's status as a champion of the people, the British seethed with anger about the blatant humiliation and intimidation of one of their officials. Hancock now had a target on his back.

## "THE MOB AGAIN TRIUMPHED"

One month later, on May 9, 1768, customs officials were still reeling from the *Lydia* incident and saw an opportunity to get even. One of Hancock's ships, *Liberty*, docked in Boston at Hancock's Wharf around sunset, which was too late to check in with the customs office. The timing was fortunate for Hancock because his ship was stocked with madeira, and he had no intention of paying taxes on the entire shipment. Waiting until nightfall, Hancock's employees illegally unloaded the majority of the wine before the customs officials could find—and tax—the goods. The next morning, customs officials ceremoniously boarded *Liberty*. Imagine their surprise and disappointment when they discovered only a tiny amount of wine aboard. Hancock paid a miniscule amount of customs on the cargo, equal to having his ship at less than a quarter capacity. A seasoned merchant like Hancock wouldn't sail with a nearly empty ship—the profits would be minimal, if any—so the customs officials knew they'd been cheated. Hancock thought he had gotten the better of the customs officials twice in five weeks—a sport he seemed to be perfecting.

But evidence—questionable as it was—to prosecute Hancock for smuggling turned up a few weeks later. A man who had been on board *Liberty* on May 9 came forward and recalled how, when he would not participate in the frenzied unloading of the wine before proper customs could be paid, he had been roughed up and detained in one of the ship's cabins. His story wasn't credible, but the British now had something they could use to prosecute Hancock. On June 8, before *Liberty* could sail back to London, two customs officers, Joseph Harrison and Benjamin Hallowell, and nearly fifty soldiers went to Hancock's Wharf. They declared Hancock's ship and all of its cargo to be property of the Crown. They towed *Liberty* through the harbor and out to the fifty-gun British man-of-war *Romney*, where it was to be guarded by the British. Fortuitously, *Romney* had arrived in Boston only a couple of weeks prior in an effort to enforce the customs duties.

Because they remained loyal to one of their favorite guys in town, the seizure of *Liberty* sent Boston's rebels into a rage. A crowd formed down at the wharf while the ship was being hauled away. Dockworkers were tough men used to hard, physical labor and would relish an opportunity to release some anger or boredom—especially on the meddling customs agents. As the customs officials seized Hancock's ship, five hundred men on the dock pelted them with rocks, bricks and stones, even trying to reach *Romney* with their objects. The mob then grabbed Harrison and Hallowell and beat them up, leaving them with "many wounds & Bruses," according to Bernard. Some mob members were inspired to new heights of destruction when they dragged a boat owned by Harrison out of the harbor water. They lugged it through the streets of Boston about a half mile. Hauling the barge up to Boston Common, they set the boat on fire. The blaze from the burning barge was not far from Hancock's mansion, sending a clear message about what would happen to others who messed with Hancock and his *Liberty*.[34]

"The Mob again triumphed; the day as well as the Night were now their own," recalled Peter Oliver, a notably biased source, but not necessarily an unreliable one. For it was true. The mob was back in Boston and demonstrated the lengths it would go to oppose the Crown and its officials. Bernard warned Harrison and Hallowell that he could not protect them, so they hid out on Castle Island, a few miles from Boston. In a newspaper article written by Samuel Adams, he justified the mob activity. He asked rhetorically, "Can any one be surprized, that when property was violently seized, under a pretence of law…that such ill-time, violent, and unheard of proceedings, should excite the resentment even of the better sort of people in town." This response echoed the Stamp Act riots against Oliver, when the mob was an accepted institution committed to righting the wrongs inflicted by the British. People ignored mob force in Boston at their own peril.[35]

Hancock was bleeding money with his ship sitting idle under British custody—he only made money by importing and exporting goods. He was eager to cut a deal to return to profitability. On June 11, at Hancock's request, his lawyer brokered a compromise with the customs agents, promising that if they would return his ship, Hancock would be available for any smuggling charges and try to calm the mob. Hancock accepted the deal because profit was his priority—one that was not shared by other rebel leaders. Samuel Adams, James Otis Jr. and emerging rebel Joseph Warren met with Hancock and told him he got the worse end of the bargain. They didn't want one of the most popular men in Boston to tell the mob to quiet down. Furthermore, striking a deal with the British made Hancock look guilty. They persuaded Hancock not to accept the deal, and he backed out of it.

After breaking off the deal, British customs officers were more eager than ever to bring formal smuggling charges against Hancock. Hancock had embarrassed them too many times in a short period of time. General Thomas Gage, commander of all British forces in North America, hoped that by putting Hancock on trial, it "will encourage the Civil Officers of every Degree, to do their Duty without Fear, and to curb effectually the Licentious and Seditious Spirit, which has so long prevailed this Place." No less than the ability of future customs officials' work was on trial. Fortunately for Hancock, he was armed with a strong defense: his young and motivated attorney, John Adams. At the core of the case was whether Hancock, as the man in charge of his employees, knew that they had illegally unloaded

The Hancock mansion on top of Beacon Hill. The house was torn down in the 1860s. *The Miriam and Ira D. Wallach Division of Art, Prints and Photographs: Print Collection, New York Public Library.*

wine. John Adams claimed that the owner "may be asleep in his Bed, and not so much as know or dream that any Body is unshipping and landing his Wines." Hancock must have known about his employees' actions, and had likely directed it many times before, but the British had a difficult time proving that and eventually had to drop the charges. Hancock *had* smuggled in goods, but the customs officials weren't patient or smart enough to prove it. Such concessions continued to empower the rebels.[36]

# "THE MOST OBSTINATE SPIRIT OF OPPOSITION"

Bernard knew that the Crown was losing control of Boston and thought armed soldiers could help restore order and enforce the Townshend Duties. He wrote to the Crown and implied that troops were necessary in Boston but didn't come outright and request them. It would make him even less popular among rebels if it were discovered that he had requested troops. He reminded the Crown about the "defenceless State of this Government" but said he'd "leav[e] it to The Administration to determine upon Measures which they are much more able to judge." Bernard wanted the soldiers in Boston but left the decision in the hands of the Crown, so they, and not he, would look like the bad guys who ordered troops to occupy a town during peacetime.[37]

After the *Liberty* mob in June and the pleading from Bernard, the Crown decided they must act firmly to take back control of Boston. Their solution was to send two regiments of soldiers to Boston. Twelve hundred troops arrived on October 1, 1768. The soldiers made a big show of their military might when they landed at Boston's Long Wharf. They hoped that if Boston's rebels got a good look at the soldiers' organization, size and weapons, the townspeople would be cowed into behaving. The troops marched up King Street, with drums beating, fifes playing and bayonets fixed on their muskets. Cannons from several warships pointed at the town from the harbor. This behavior was more typical of entering a hostile town or fighting a battle than occupying a peaceful town of fellow British subjects. As if that wasn't enough, nearly 800 more soldiers arrived in November, bringing the total number of British soldiers in Boston to 2,000. This was in a town of 15,500 people, which included only about 3,000 adult men. With the arrival of the troops, the adult male population of this small town increased by more than 60 percent in one month, and conflict seemed imminent. It is difficult to

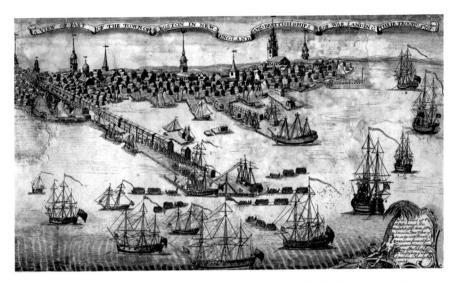

Paul Revere's depiction of the British troops' arrival in 1768. Hundreds of troops disembark at Long Wharf. *Courtesy of the American Antiquarian Society.*

imagine a scenario in which Boston would have, at best, greeted the soldiers indifferently and continued about their business. At worst—well—Bostonians had a lot of potential to make trouble.

While British officials and Loyalists in Boston may have found the soldiers a welcome sight, many colonists throughout North America shuddered at the idea of a standing, or permanent, army, in their midst. Historically, the colonies didn't have an army—they relied on the militia to fight when necessary. Standing armies were seen as dangerous because they could subject citizens to military rule and were responsible only for their own rules and dictums. They were not considered freethinking members of the community. John Hancock claimed that standing armies were often composed of men "unfit to live in civil society…who have given up their own liberties, and envy those who enjoy liberty." Samuel Adams, writing as *Vindex*, railed against the presence of an army in Boston. He argued that "the raising and keeping a standing army within the kingdom, in a time of peace…is Against Law." Parliament had enacted a military solution to what was not yet a military problem, and rebels weren't having it.[38]

Worse, Bostonians learned that the soldiers wanted to quarter in Boston. The Quartering Act of 1765 said that soldiers were required to first occupy any available barracks in public buildings. It did not call for soldiers to stay in private homes, as is commonly believed, but it did require townspeople to pay for the troops' provisions. To Bostonians, this was another form of taxation without representation, as their property was being taken without their consent. Taxes were bad enough, but having to pay for the troops' rum, for example, was really egregious. The rebels came up with a clever solution for where to put the troops.

Complying with the letter of the Quartering Act law, Boston's Town Council offered to quarter the troops at Castle Island in Boston Harbor. The council insisted that they were not going to construct any new barracks or house soldiers elsewhere until the barracks on Castle Island were first filled. Since Castle Island was technically a part of Boston, the savvy council was fulfilling its duty by providing shelter in the town. But those barracks were on an island three miles from the coast of Boston, defeating the entire purpose of occupying a town. After all, Castle Island was so far from Boston that in the midst of the *Liberty* riots, this was where customs officials retired in safety. General Gage noted, "at Such a Distance from the Town of Boston," the soldiers would serve little purpose. While both sides waited for the soldiers' housing to be sorted out, Bernard told one regiment that they could camp on Boston Common and another could stay in a large building a few yards from Boston Common, called the Manufactory House.[39]

Constructed in 1754, the Manufactory House was 140 feet long and 2 stories high and had a sizeable cellar, making it a good place to house soldiers. It was originally established as a business venture where poor, sick or homeless weavers and spinners would live and work in the building while producing wool and linen. The house didn't make enough money to sustain itself and eventually became property of Massachusetts. By the time the British troops arrived, only a few weavers and squatters lived there. In early October, a British officer went to the Manufactory House and "with an order from the Governor," requested that the occupants leave. Instead of complying, the residents were defiant—"the doors were barr'd and bolted against the [soldiers]." The town sheriff, Stephen Greenleaf, and Lieutenant

Castle Island was in desperate need of repairs, but Loyalists and royal officials still chose it as their frequent sanctuary. *Library of Congress.*

Boston Common in 1768 with British troops and tents in the center of the park. John Hancock's mansion is at the top of Beacon Hill, as is the beacon that acted as a warning device. *The Miriam and Ira D. Wallach Division of Art, Prints and Photographs: Print Collection, New York Public Library.*

Governor Thomas Hutchinson arrived and demanded that the servants vacate the premises. One informed occupant told them that they didn't have the authority to evict the residents because it had not been properly approved by the General Court.[40]

Greenleaf returned to the building the next day "accompanied by the soldiery" and forcibly tried to gain access to the building through the cellar. Greenleaf tangled with a weaver and remained locked out while some of the troops took control of the cellar, thinking they might be able to occupy the building that way. Redcoats also surrounded the building and stood guard. "All persons were forbid[den] from going in and out," reported a local newspaper. The British soldiers hoped to starve the residents out of the Manufactory House. When the hungry residents finally and desperately evacuated, the soldiers planned to rush in and take over the building. The redcoats just had to be patient.[41]

The residents had been trapped inside the house going on two days, and children and adults alike suffered. A newspaper reported that there were "children at the windows crying for bread." To assuage their hunger, a sympathetic baker came to the Manufactory House to deliver bread to the people confined inside. The soldiers guarding the building prevented him from entering. Undeterred, Bostonians took the matter into their own hands. Townspeople threw the loaves of bread into the open windows right over the heads of the soldiers. The soldiers hadn't been in Boston a month before they got a taste of Boston rebels' determination and creativity. To retaliate, British soldiers assaulted some of the participating townspeople, but no one suffered any severe injuries. "Loss of blood, but no lives," was reported. This was the first blood shed in a conflict between townspeople and redcoats.[42]

The standoff lasted several days before the British eventually gave up and removed the troops from the perimeter of the Manufactory House. A newspaper wrote, "With the trifling loss of…honour and reputation—the troops were withdrawn under cover of night." British authority in Boston was being dismantled piece by piece. Like Oliver's resignation, the Stamp Act repeal and dropping smuggling charges against Hancock, abandoning the Manufactory House represented another devastating British compliance. Boston rebels were proving that they would take Crown employees to the mat.[43]

Hindsight, of course, offers us a clear view. With every British repeal or withdrawal, Parliament and Crown officials allowed Boston to grow dangerously bolder. But those in London didn't know that. They underestimated the rebels' will—partly because they were misinformed by their own agents in the colonies. For example, General Gage wrote to Lord Hillsborough about the standoff at the Manufactory House and acknowledged that the soldiers had tried to take the Manufactory House but said that it was "a little Disturbance of no Consequence." He failed to mention that the British were not able to occupy the house and had to withdraw the troops from the perimeter. Gage played down the clash to assure the Crown that he was in control. For years to come, his letters would often omit the details that might make his troops look bad or weak. It would ultimately haunt him.[44]

Despite his deceptive reports, Gage seemed to know that a dangerous energy was boiling in Boston. He admitted that the rebels possess "the most obstinate Spirit of Opposition, to every Measure of Government." And the soldiers hadn't yet been effective in taming Boston. Worse, sending troops to occupy Boston gave townspeople a visible enemy—every redcoat that now walked down the street was seen as a threat to their liberty. The showdown at the Manufactory House represented the first violent confrontation between the townspeople and redcoats, but there would be more headaches ahead for Gage. The "obstinate spirit" of Boston was only heating up.[45]

# FROM PAST TO PRESENT

## LIBERTY BOWL

*We are fortunate that this bowl still exists today in a place where it can be admired by the public. This bowl is owned by the Museum of Fine Arts, Boston and is housed in its Art of the Americas wing, fittingly in front of John Singleton Copley's portrait of Paul Revere. Fifteen members of the Sons of Liberty commissioned Revere to make the bowl, and their names are inscribed around the top. The museum's presentation allows you to view the work of art on all sides, where you can admire Revere's craftsmanship. Notice one side of the bowl where it praises the Massachusetts House members who voted not to rescind the circular letter and were "undaunted by the insolent Menaces of Villains in Power." Bowls of this size would often be receptacles for punch—which was made with rum, tea and spices—and passed around from man to man to drink out of.*

## CASTLE ISLAND

*Today, Castle Island is no longer an island. It was connected to the mainland in the 1930s, making it accessible by car. The fort that exists there now is not from the colonial period, as that one was run down even in the 1760s. The current fort, Fort Independence, was constructed in the mid-nineteenth century and is the eighth fort to be on the island. Castle Island is a pleasant place to visit in the summer and has lots of outdoor space. When you're there, turn back to*

The view of Castle Island from Boston Harbor today. *Public domain.*

*look at the city behind you and imagine how frustrating it would have been if you were a British soldier who was told you had to stay there and try to protect Boston from itself.*

## SITE OF THE MANUFACTORY HOUSE

*There isn't much to look at anymore, but you can go to the site where the standoff happened and view two landmarks from that time period to help orient you. On the corner of Tremont Street and Hamilton Place you'll find Suffolk University Law School. Take a few steps down Hamilton Place and look to your left. You'll see a green sign on the wall of the law school identifying the site of the Manufactory House. (Those green signs are posted by the Bostonian Society and are all over the city.) Across the street is the Granary Burying Ground and Boston Common, both of which existed during the tumult. Use those markers to imagine a fairly large two-story house with redcoats trying to take it over and loaves of bread comically being thrown over their heads.*

The corner of Hamilton Place and Tremont Street with the Manufactory House site plaque. The Granary Burying Ground is visible across the street. *Photograph by the author.*

# 4

# Six People in Ten Days

*Key Player: The Charismatic Joseph Warren*

Bostonians were on edge. Around eight o'clock in the morning on Monday, October 31, 1768, townspeople could hear drummers sounding the "dead beat." It seemed to be coming from near Boston Common. And then, figures came into view. A young man dressed all in white appeared—ghostlike—at the top of Beacon Hill. He was followed by several soldiers as they all marched down the hill to Boston Common. The young man was positioned in front of a firing squad. Was this actually happening in front of so many people? The soldiers lifted their guns. Aimed. And shot the man in white. They left his body for dead. Right there in Boston's public park. His name was Private Richard Ames. His crime was desertion. Apparently, even the British soldiers didn't want to be in Boston.

Within the first two weeks of their arrival, no doubt inspired by the unwelcome reception from the townspeople and the vast countryside where they could hide, over forty British soldiers deserted their military positions. The threat of desertion was so real that the British set up a guardhouse on the Neck with guards checking every cart and carriage that passed through. The punishments for desertion were severe—floggings and death—and could be done in public, like that of Ames. One newspaper reported that his was "the first execution of the kind ever seen in this town." It was a shocking sight to Bostonians, but probably not for the soldiers, who were used to brutal punishments.[46]

Being in Boston was a wretched experience for the soldiers. Many Bostonians despised and resented the king's troops who occupied their town and made no secret of showing it. General Gage reported to London that since the redcoats arrived, Bostonians have "laid every Snare to entrap and distress" the soldiers, while insulting them daily. Some British officers claimed that it was "unsafe for an officer or soldier to walk the streets." They even claimed to have overheard several Bostonians threaten "that they would kill all the officers in the town." For the redcoats, Boston could be seen as a small, claustrophobic town that offered little relief from the aggressive provincialism and disrespect for British authority. For the rebels, the soldiers were not simply a police force that had come to shut down their spirit of resistance. Many believed that the troops' presence was part of a concerted effort to take away Boston's liberties.[47]

Bostonians had good reason to be tormented by the troops' occupation. Going about daily business in Boston now seemed more dangerous, annoying or difficult because of the soldiers. Samuel Adams, who dramatically claimed that the soldiers were "stationed in our very bowels," was troubled because townspeople couldn't walk through their streets unmolested anymore. "Affronted in the night as well as the day by soldiers arm'd with muskets and fix'd bayonets," he poignantly asked, "Are these the blessings of government?" The soldiers also offended Bostonians' Puritan sense of piety because the soldiers were too loud on the Sabbath, their holy day. Townspeople complained that "serious people at public worship were greatly disturbed with drums beating and fifes playing." Bostonians asked the officers to stop this noise, especially near the churches, but it continued—with soldiers even orchestrating a horse race on Boston Common on a Sunday in 1769. The soldiers also drank too much alcohol. Soldiers received a ration of alcohol from the army—often beer or rum—and supplemented that with local offerings. Townspeople complained that soldiers were frequently drunk, especially because "distilled spirits are so cheap and plenty." (As the leading rum producer in the thirteen colonies, Boston had easy access to rum, so it wasn't just the soldiers who imbibed. It made for a convenient complaint, though.)[48]

Between their fear of standing armies and their hatred of the soldiers, Bostonians felt pushed to the brink. Elected officials wanted to punish the person they felt was responsible for bringing the soldiers here: Governor Bernard. (His careful attempts to look like he hadn't requested troops were unsuccessful.) In June 1769, the House of Representatives of Massachusetts sent a petition to the king requesting that Bernard "be for ever removed from the Government of his Province." The petition aired seventeen grievances, including that Bernard falsely portrayed Boston to his agents in London as being overrun by unruly mobs. The House complained that he "has very injuriously represented your Majesty's loving subjects of this Colony." The House also griped that Bernard tried to quarter troops in Boston without first filling the barracks on Castle Island. In doing so, he had "rendered his Administration odious to the whole body of the people, and has entirely alienated their affections from him." Conveniently for Boston, Lord Hillsborough had decided earlier that year to recall Bernard from his post.[49]

The unpopular royal governor of Massachusetts, Francis Bernard. *The Miriam and Ira D. Wallach Division of Art, Prints and Photographs: Print Collection, New York Public Library.*

Bernard departed Boston on August 1, 1769, which, as expected, was a day of celebration in Boston. The townspeople had gotten their way again. Even though it was not their petition that led to Bernard's removal, Bostonians felt they ruled the day, much like their celebration over the Stamp Act repeal three years earlier. The Sons of Liberty hosted an enormous dinner to celebrate and sang songs lampooning Bernard. One song had been penned by an up-and-coming rebel, Dr. Benjamin Church, who had a sharp mind for political satire. He would have plenty more material to generate in the coming years because the next royal governor of Massachusetts would be the man Boston rebels loved to hate: Thomas Hutchinson.

## HOMESPUN HARASSMENT

Bernard leaving Massachusetts was a victory, but the Townshend Duties were still on the books, and rebels—not just those from Boston—wanted to render them meaningless. To do that, colonies throughout North American agreed to a nonimportation agreement, beginning in January 1769, that prohibited merchants from importing British goods. For the boycott to succeed, clothing imported from London had to be seen as unfashionable, and homemade clothing had to become a new, desirable trend. Fashion was becoming political. This was a brilliant way to involve men and women, rich and poor, in the political process. Thomas Hutchinson thought that the boycott was the most defiant colonial action to date because it began with merchants, moved to traders and then trickled down to everyday members of the community. This gave ordinary people an awareness of British policies that Parliament had not intended. Women in Boston were particularly crucial to this nonimportation effort, as they began spinning their own cloth to fashion their families' wardrobes. This new clothing was earnestly called homespun, and it became a sign of patriotism to make one's own garments and shun British fashions.[50]

Not everyone in Boston heeded the nonimportation agreement, and they paid dearly. Merchants who continued to import British goods found themselves frequently harassed. Mobs broke such merchants' windows and vandalized their signs. One merchant, Nathaniel Rogers, the nephew of Thomas Hutchinson, was targeted by rebels for over a year. Rebels threatened Rogers physically, smashed his home's windows and—this tactic is truly disgusting—smeared his house with a mixture of feces and urine. This was not the first time they graced a home with such vile filth. It was known as "Hillsborough paint," named for Lord Hillsborough. The names of merchants who continued to import British goods were also printed in newspapers and labeled as enemies. This included the Hutchinsons, the wealthy merchant family headed by Richard Clarke and Theophilus Lillie.

Theophilus Lillie, a merchant with a shop on Hanover Street in the North End, went one day from being on notice in newspapers as an importer to having a crowd at his doorstep. On February 22, 1770, a group of people gathered in front of Lillie's store because he was selling items imported from England. He claimed that he had purchased the goods before the nonimportation agreement began, but his protests fell on deaf ears. The crowd wanted to humiliate Lillie and prevent anyone from entering the store to buy the damned British goods. At first glance, the scene was fairly comical. The crowd included mostly schoolchildren and teenaged apprentices, people with enough time on their hands to get into some mischief. On top of a cart, they had a massive, painted likeness of Lillie's head (which must have taken considerable effort to create beforehand). The group also carried protest signs and spilled out into the middle of the street.

The tableau stopped being funny when a British customs officer named Ebenezer Richardson stopped by. Richardson was a neighbor of Lillie and widely known for being a jerk around Boston. As one newspaper reported, he had "a most abandon'd Character." His poor character wasn't just the prejudice of rebels. While married to his wife, he had gotten her sister pregnant. He also had worked as a customs informant—the most contemptible of jobs because he would tip off customs agents about smugglers. True to this abandoned character, Richardson couldn't help himself when he saw the crowd and "soon became a Party in the Affair." Richardson tried to grab the signs from the children and yelled at everyone to disperse. He was ultimately successful in moving the crowd from Lillie's storefront, but he had merely shifted their attention.[51]

By sticking his nose in their protests, Richardson made himself more interesting to the crowd than Lillie. As Richardson walked home, the crowd followed and taunted him. He made it inside his home while the group stood outside. With the bravery that can come only from inside the safety of one's dwelling, he and his wife began shouting at the crowd. Such tactics certainly weren't going to scare people away—the Richardsons' aggression only incited them. The throng responded by throwing trash at his house. Richardson returned the favor and threw trash onto the crowd. The group then threw more dangerous objects—rocks and stones—at his house, breaking some of his windows. It was mostly a nonthreatening situation until Richardson snapped.

Richardson grabbed his musket, leaned out his window and fired birdshot into the crowd. Two people were hit. The first, Samuel "Sammy" Gore, was a nineteen-year-old man who was shot several times in both of his legs and one of his hands, which would ultimately remain without some of its feeling for his entire life. The other person Richardson hit was a boy about eleven years of age, Christopher Snider, who was mortally wounded. He suffered several shots, one of which pierced a lung. This shot killed him. His blood soaked into the winter-hardened grounds of Boston. An eleven-year-old child was dead at the hands of a British customs official.[52]

The wounded boys were taken to a doctor who was developing into an ardent rebel. Dr. Joseph Warren removed the bullets from Sammy Gore but could do no more than perform an autopsy of Snider. For a rising rebel leader, staring at the lifeless body of a boy who was in the wrong place at the wrong time—surely Snider had not been causing Richardson too much trouble—would have likely increased Warren's hatred of British officials and the soldiers. Warren was just twenty-eight years of age when Richardson shot into the crowd—a formative time to see firsthand how dangerous the lackeys of the Crown could be.

# THE CHARISMATIC DOCTOR, JOSEPH WARREN

Despite his youth, Joseph Warren had one of the most respected and busiest medical practices in Boston, even tending to John Hancock's health. After graduating from Harvard and apprenticing with a prominent doctor in Boston, he set up his practice at the age of twenty-three. During the smallpox outbreak in Boston in 1764, Warren was trusted to inoculate many residents, including John Adams, saving many lives with the proven, but risky, procedure. For a short time in 1767, Warren even crossed over rebel lines to care for Thomas Hutchinson and the ousted Stamp Act collector Andrew Oliver. They may have been trying to woo this amiable doctor to the Loyalist side, for he was a big get.

As a popular doctor, Warren was part of an extensive network of people in Boston. He knew and had intimate access to varied levels of society. Furthering those connections, Warren joined St. Andrew's Lodge, the largest Masonic group in Boston, which also counted John Hancock and the well-connected silversmith Paul Revere as members. He would later become its grand master. Warren also was a member of the North End Caucus, one of the most politically significant groups in Boston at this time. The North End Caucus's members included Samuel and John Adams; street agitator William Molineux; Dr. Benjamin Church, known at this time for his political satire; and Revere. These clubs helped Warren get to know and become informally involved in politics, for he wouldn't be elected to political office until 1774. But one didn't need to be voted into political office at this time to be influential. Warren impressed the men around him with his knack for propaganda and leadership.

Physically, Warren looked the part of a charismatic and influential leader. He was taller than most of his contemporaries and quite handsome, if baby-faced. He had fair skin and hair, which he often kept in horizontal rolls, the rage at that time. Copley's portrait of Warren shows a confident and approachable man. Warren's appeal drew the attention of a wealthy teenaged woman, Elizabeth Hooten, whom he married in 1764. Her family money greatly advanced Warren's social position at a key time because he had just been starting out in medicine. When Elizabeth died in 1773, she left behind four children and a thirty-one-year-old widower. With his good looks and charm, Warren was not at a loss for female attention and found at least one woman, but likely two, to keep him company in the next couple of years.[53]

Warren had the connections and appeal of a leader, but he also succeeded in acting the part. If such a thing can be measured, Warren was one of

John Singleton Copley's portrait of Joseph Warren captures his broad appeal to Bostonians. Completed around 1765, Warren appears welcoming and genteel. *Museum of Fine Arts, Boston.*

the bravest men in Boston's rebel circles. He would stay behind in Boston when Samuel Adams and John Hancock needed to flee town—making him a potential target for Gage or soldiers. And he was the only one of the rebel leaders to actually fight on the front lines alongside the men he called on to fight. The only one. He was also a hard worker, evidenced by his thriving medical practice, which included two apprentices and seeing nearly twenty patients a day. This was a man who could handle pressure, diagnose a situation quickly and stand in the line of fire. The rebels were lucky to have him.

## "ABUSING THE SOLDIERY"

Snider's funeral happened a few days after the shooting and was a town-wide spectacle designed to incite anger and unity among Bostonians. It began, appropriately, at the Liberty Tree. Several hundred boys marched two by two through the cold winter chill for more than a half mile. Over two thousand adults marched behind them. Carriages and chaises extended beyond the people, comprising what Hutchinson imagined to be the "largest funeral perhaps ever known in America." A columnist in a local newspaper called Snider a "little Hero and first Martyr to the noble Cause."[54]

Snider's death made a difficult situation for the soldiers even worse. Captain Thomas Preston, who was stationed in Boston and would soon be at the center of one of the most famous events in American history, commented that "the utter hatred of the Inhabitants [of Boston] to the Troops increased daily." And Bostonians didn't just hate the troops; they were, according to Preston, "constantly provoking & abusing the Soldiery." The soldiers were grown men who were unlikely to stand for such abuse before they eventually lost their tempers. It would happen a week after Snider's death.[55]

On Friday, March 2, a British soldier, Patrick Walker, was strolling through John Gray's ropewalks in the South End. Walker asked the rope workers if they had some work he could do for extra cash. Soldiers were underpaid and frequently sought work in Boston to supplement their income. Samuel Gray, a rope worker, and no relation to John Gray, told Walker that if he wanted extra work, he could clean out their latrine. That's a fine eighteenth-century insult. And it came from a potentially dangerous man. Rope workers were tough and were not to be treated cavalierly, even if—in your mind—one of them had just grievously disrespected you. Walker should have heeded his surname and kept on walking.

Instead, Walker picked a fight with Gray. And lost. With wounded pride, Walker sulked back to the barracks. About twenty minutes later, he returned to the ropewalk with eight or nine of his comrades, feeling much braver. Samuel Gray was likely amused to see Walker a second time. Walker and his entourage picked another fight with Gray, who had grabbed some of his buddies to join in. The vengeful soldiers "were again worsted" in this confrontation. Undeterred, the losers went back to the barracks and returned again (again!) a short time later with thirty to forty soldiers armed with "clubs and cutlasses." When this crowd arrived, rope workers within shouting distance banded together for the brawl. It was a prizefight—about forty vengeful soldiers with a fighting record of 0-2 versus the undefeated, toughest men in Boston. The rope workers would again carry the final fight, leaving the soldiers with "considerable bruises." For the third time in one day, British soldiers got clobbered by Bostonians. It was unlikely to be the last word.[56]

The atmosphere was so tense that another clash in Boston felt imminent. A Loyalist said that after the waterfront fight, "the soldiers wished for another engagement to revenge themselves on the rope-makers." Matthew Killroy, a soldier who had participated in the large brawl, clearly wanted another shot at the Bostonians. He was overheard saying that "he would never miss an opportunity of firing upon the inhabitants." Thomas Hutchinson predicted in February (even before the rope workers pummeled the redcoats) that chaos might break out in mid-March when the General Court was in session in Boston. Hutchinson's prediction was off by just a few days.[57]

Monday, March 5, was an active night in Boston, with many people milling about or causing trouble. Soldiers were patrolling the streets, which were covered in several inches of snow. Small fights broke out between men and soldiers in the late afternoon and into the evening. Later that night—around nine o'clock—bells from three separate churches started to ring. When the people of Boston and other colonial towns heard church bells, it was often a warning sign—of a fire, perhaps, or of a fight. This time it was a fight. It broke out in front of the customs house on King Street—steps from the Old State House. King Street was a busy street in Boston, packed with taverns and shops, so activity there wasn't surprising.

The fight began when a young man, brave with drink, came upon Private Hugh White, the lone British soldier guarding the customs house. The drunk insulted the soldier, as was common practice in Boston. The cranky soldier took the butt of his musket and struck the guy in the face. The young man fell down, started crying and yelled out to King Street that he'd been assaulted by a soldier. He grabbed some friends, and they insulted White and threw snowballs at him. The situation escalated, as the ringing bells brought more people into the streets. A crowd soon formed in front of the customs house.

This was not a genteel crowd, as many members of the group consisted of drunk laborers. John Adams famously referred to this crowd as a group of "a motley rabble of saucy boys, negroes, and mullatoes, Irish teagues and outlandish jack tarrs." The nearby taverns on King Street contributed to the intoxicated mob. There were now about thirty men encircling and taunting White, who jabbed his bayonet into the crowd to keep them at a distance. As the mob continued to grow, White called for backup, and seven soldiers and one officer, Captain Thomas Preston, arrived from nearby barracks.[58]

The situation was combustible. Nine beleaguered redcoats faced the mob. They loaded their muskets, which incited the crowd, now numbering perhaps as many as two hundred men. The mob taunted the soldiers to fire. Captain Preston heard the crowd yell, "Come on you rascals, you bloody backs, you Lobster scoundrels, fire if you dare, G-d damn you, fire & be damn'd." The crowd's bravery partly owed to the fact that soldiers could not fire on them without orders from a civil magistrate. No magistrate was in sight. The crowd also threw objects at the soldiers—snowballs, oyster shells and trash—whatever they could find on the street.[59]

Then, in an instant, everything changed. One member of the mob, some say a dockworker named Crispus Attucks, threw a snowball that struck a redcoat, Private Hugh Montgomery, in the shoulder. Witnesses also claimed the object was a "large stick" or a "piece of ice." When the object hit Montgomery's shoulder, his gun discharged into the crowd. The other soldiers heard the shot and thought that if one soldier had fired, perhaps they were to shoot as well. "One after the other," the soldiers fired into the crowd. At the end of the shooting, three men lay dead, including Attucks, in the center of King Street. Two men would die later of their wounds. Six men were injured. This event became known by colonists as the "bloody Massacre." We know it today as the Boston Massacre.[60]

It was an absolutely stunning crescendo to the violence of the past ten days. In less than twenty minutes, the soldiers had lost control of themselves and shot into a crowd of rowdy—but unarmed—Bostonians. Thomas Hutchinson, acting quite bravely, arrived at the scene shortly after the shooting and appeared at the balcony of the Old State House. He wrote that "the people were enraged to a very great degree and could not be pacified" until he told the people that he would look into the matter impartially and completely. This, along with the corralling of redcoats away from the crowd, caused the mob to disperse—but only until morning. The next morning, Boston's leaders and three thousand townspeople confronted Hutchinson. The crowd, naturally, demanded that the troops leave Boston. The pressure became so immense for the troops to leave town that, except for those awaiting trial, the soldiers were shipped out on March 10.[61]

The departure of the troops didn't mitigate the most chilling part of the March 5 shooting. For the Boston Massacre wasn't simply nine random soldiers firing on an anonymous crowd. Some of the men on both sides of the shooting knew one another and not only that, but had reason to hate one another. Samuel Gray, the rope worker who had initially insulted Walker at the docks just three days earlier, had been shot dead in the shooting. Many townspeople believed that the soldier who shot him had also participated in the fight. One witness even claimed to have seen the soldier pointing at Gray in the crowd before firing. And three of the nine soldiers at the Massacre, including Matthew Killroy, had participated in that massive brawl. The hatred between redcoats and some Bostonians had gotten personal and ugly. These relationships would be the crux of the murder trial for the British soldiers.

# MALICIOUS MOB

Loyalists, including General Gage, worried that the soldiers would not be able to "have a fair and impartial Tryal for their Lives," for Gage claimed that "no Jury will be found in Boston, who will dare…to give any other Verdict" than guilty. It didn't help the soldiers' case that rebels had gotten to work on propaganda surrounding the event. Paul Revere famously engraved an image (or rather plagiarized much of an image by John Singleton Copley's half brother, Henry Pelham) of the Boston Massacre. It is notable for its inaccuracy. It shows British troops resembling a firing squad shooting at a passive, small and unarmed crowd. Prescott is behind them raising his sword to command the troops to fire and behind him is the customs house, which Revere cheekily renamed "Butcher's Hall." Joseph Warren also helped to write an account of the massacre, blaming the soldiers for attacking peaceful townspeople. The soldiers did have one thing going for them: an excellent defense team. Their lawyers were Harvard-educated and rebels, who had surprisingly agreed to defend the soldiers in an effort to show that Massachusetts was not without law.[62]

John Adams and Josiah Quincy Jr., the redcoats' attorneys, insisted that Preston be charged separately from the soldiers. They were concerned that if the officer was tried with the soldiers, the jury would conflate all

Paul Revere's engraving of the Boston Massacre. The Old State House anchors the background and represents one of the only accurate components of this scene. *Library of Congress.*

the men as equally guilty. The defense got their wish, and Preston's trial began in August 1770. Adams and Quincy had a simple defense: Preston never ordered any soldier to fire. Witness after witness confirmed this fact. Even Samuel Adams, who wrote constantly about the trial for the local newspapers and desperately wanted the soldiers convicted, claimed that the soldiers were restricted from firing until Preston "first gave them orders: Yet contrary to those very rules they all did fire." Witnesses confirmed hearing the word "fire" being shouted, but they identified those as taunts from the crowd, not from the captain. Preston was found not guilty.[63]

Since Preston had not ordered the soldiers to fire, the defense needed to prove that the soldiers had just cause to shoot into the crowd. According to British law, if a person is physically assaulted, that person can fight back—even shooting his attacker. John Adams explained that "as soon as you touch" a man and he then stabs you "thro' the heart it is but manslaughter." If Adams could prove that the soldiers had been assaulted first by the mob, it would reduce a potential murder sentence to manslaughter. Before hearing testimony, Judge Edmund Trowbridge instructed the jurors: "Malice is the grand criterion that distinguishes murder from all other homicide." Since there was no doubt that some of the soldiers had killed townspeople, the questions for the jury became which of the soldiers killed the victims, whether the soldiers had been attacked before shooting and if they fired with malicious intent.[64]

A young and stoic John Adams. *The Miriam and Ira D. Wallach Division of Art, Prints and Photographs: Print Collection, New York Public Library.*

Over the course of the trial, two of the soldiers were identified as having fired fatal shots into the mob. Hugh Montgomery was known to have killed Attucks, and Matthew Killroy was believed to have killed Gray. Because it wasn't known who of the other six soldiers had fired the shots that killed the three other victims, they could not be convicted. Montgomery had a better case than Killroy because he benefitted from witness testimony. Richard Palmes swore that "something resembling ice" hit Montgomery, who stepped back after the impact and then fired. If Montgomery had been hit by a rebel first, there could be no malice in his firing. Rather, his shooting into the crowd was a response to being hit. Therefore, under British law, Montgomery could not be convicted of murder.[65]

The lack of malice would be a harder case to prove for Killroy (an unfortunate name for a man on trial for murder), since he was at the ropewalk fight a few days before and had been overheard saying he wouldn't miss an opportunity to shoot Boston's townspeople. Furthermore, there was no firm evidence proving that Gray had first assaulted Killroy before he shot into the crowd. But Judge Trowbridge claimed, "if the assault upon [Killroy]...would justify firing and killing...that would not inhance the killing to murder." It became very difficult for the jury—which had no Bostonians sitting on it—to convict Killroy of murder because the crowd had clearly assaulted him and the other soldiers first. At the end of a long trial (long by colonial standards at just over a week, but nothing like the duration of high-profile trials today), Montgomery and Killroy were both found guilty of manslaughter, not murder. Their punishment was to have their thumbs branded. It was not the outcome that most rebels had hoped for.[66]

Governor Hutchinson probably thought he would have an angry and unruly town on his hands after the Boston Massacre trial. After six people had been killed by British officials in ten days, Boston could and should have been more explosive than ever. Yet many Bostonians shockingly accepted the outcome of the trial. With the troops gone and most taxes off the books—the Townshend Duties had been repealed, except for the tax on tea—Bostonians seemed to retire their hatred of the British Empire. And for the next few years, Boston went into a lull, as there wasn't much to complain about. For rebel leaders, it was difficult to get townspeople riled up when life seemed normal again and there was no immediate threat to their liberties, safety or pocketbooks. It took a few years, but it would be Hutchinson, yet again, who would give Samuel Adams a cause to rally people around.

## FROM PAST TO PRESENT

### BOSTON MASSACRE SITE

*Along the Freedom Trail, there is a stone circle in front of the Old State House that says, "Site of the Boston Massacre." That circle does not accurately mark where the shooting happened and has moved locations over the years. The shooting actually happened about fifty feet in front of the marker when facing east, in the middle of the busy intersection of State and Congress Streets. The marker's current location makes for a safer photo opportunity, so that's the best place to visit. When you stand in that area, imagine several inches of snow on the ground, church bells furiously ringing and an agitated town coming out to see what the fuss was about. And then picture an angry confrontation suddenly turning deadly as muskets fire and five men fall.*

This stone circle is the city's (mislocated) marker for the site of the Boston Massacre. State Street extends in the background. *Photograph by the author.*

## FANEUIL HALL

*Built in 1742, this building served as both a market and town hall for Boston. Ebenezer Richardson was brought here after shooting Snider, and the funeral for the victims of the Boston Massacre was held here. It was in a part of town known as Dock Square and nearly waterfront property, for the shoreline was much closer. When you visit Faneuil Hall today, know that the building's current size is much larger than it was in the eighteenth century because, in 1805, famed architect Charles Bulfinch expanded the building. Behind Faneuil Hall, you'll also see Quincy Market, North Market and South Market, which were erected on landfill in the mid-1820s.*

Faneuil Hall today, with a statue of Samuel Adams in front. *Courtesy of Ryan Shelby.*

# 5

# PARTY WITH ABANDON, PUNISH WITH ABANDON

## *Key Player: A Steely and Stubborn Richard Clarke*

H e'd done it again. Hutchinson, Boston's villain, made it just too easy for rebels to hate him. Letters written in the 1760s between Hutchinson, Andrew Oliver and customs officials were leaked to rebel leaders in the spring of 1773. They were pretty damning. Hutchinson wrote that there "must be an abridgment of what are called English liberties." Worse, Hutchinson wasn't sure that a colony "3,000 miles distant from the parent state" could enjoy the same freedoms as the mother country. He wished "further restraint of liberty rather than the connexion with the parent state should be broken." Hutchinson was willing to sell out some of his and his constituents' freedoms to remain under the rule of the British Empire. These letters confirmed to rebels that Hutchinson had, for years, been plotting against them. Samuel Adams claimed the letters "show that the plan for the ruin of American Liberty was laid by a few men born & educated amongst us, & governed by Avarice and a Lust of power." Adams knew that these letters must be made public in the hopes of finally awakening Bostonians.[67]

You see, after the Boston Massacre trial, things had gotten kind of soft around Boston. Most of the British troops had been sent out of Boston, and all but one of the Townshend Duties had been repealed. Those concessions were enough to satisfy much of the populace. The major cities in the colonies, including Boston, New York and Philadelphia, had also given up on the nonimportation agreement, as the firm resolve against drinking tea from 1769 all but waned. Lord Hillsborough even wrote to Hutchinson about "the tranquility which has been happily restored to [Boston]." It seemed like a different town than the rambunctious one of the late 1760s. Samuel Adams and Joseph Warren were not happy about it.[68]

In November 1772, Adams and Warren set up a Committee of Correspondence, whose goal was to communicate with the other colonies in North America. Boston would keep other colonies apprised of information related to Massachusetts in exchange for other colonies doing the same. This way, Boston's problems became Maryland's problems and those of North Carolina, too. But the Committee of Correspondence's letters and updates would matter little if there was no immediate threat to the colonists. Hutchinson viewed the committee—whose very existence irked him—as a sad and ineffective substitute for mob violence. He cattily wrote that rebel leaders "have not been able to revive the old spirit of mobbing, and the only dependence left is to keep up a correspondence through the province by committees of the several towns, which is such a foolish scheme that they must necessarily make themselves ridiculous." Hutchinson may have thought the committee was silly, but that was before they had real news to pass on.[69]

Hutchinson's letters became a gift to the "ridiculous" Committee of Correspondence because they were an opportunity to remind colonists of the ubiquitous threats to their liberties. Massachusetts's own governor advocated for his colonists to have fewer liberties than those living in Great Britain! It was exactly what Adams needed to rouse rebels. In June 1773, not only did Adams share the contraband Hutchinson letters, but he published them in the *Boston Gazette*, where they could be reprinted in other colonies' newspapers. The rebels then took it a step further and wrote to London requesting that Hutchinson, like Governor Bernard before him, be removed from office. Rebels' suspicions about Hutchinson being against his own people had now been verified with proof from his own mouth (and quill), and Boston could no longer stomach having him in charge.

# TAXING TEA (AND BOSTONIANS' PATIENCE)

Ignorant to the letters and drama swirling in Boston, in May 1773, Parliament made the issue with Hutchinson look like a small spat between siblings. The British East India Company, which controlled Great Britain's tea trade, was on the verge of economic collapse. It had a surplus of tea—exceeding sixteen million pounds—rotting in its warehouses. In an effort to get rid of the tea, Parliament passed the Tea Act, which required colonists in North America to buy their tea only from the British East India Company. It also imposed a tax on this tea. To make the tea and tax more palatable, Parliament slashed the price of the East India Company tea to two shillings per pound, which cost less than the Dutch tea they typically smuggled. Parliament then sneakily added a nominal tax on their tea—three pence a pound, which still made their tea cheaper than their illegal competitors, but the lower price wasn't fooling anyone. The Tea Act, any way you looked at it, was bad news.

Throughout the North American colonies, rebels hated the idea of the Tea Act for two primary reasons. First, the rebels knew that this reduced price on tea wouldn't last forever. By charging less for East India Company tea, Parliament would drive out any competitors, and once they were gone, Parliament could freely increase the price of their tea. People rightfully feared a monopoly. Second, the colonists resented that they would be the ones to bail out the East India Company—an enterprise and problem they felt they had nothing to do with. Many in Boston had a third reason to resent the Tea Act: Thomas Hutchinson and his incestuous family were going to profit from it. Hutchinson had money invested in the East India Company, so he was going to make money when they sold the tea. Even worse, two of Hutchinson's sons were consignees of the tea, which meant they would be personally responsible for collecting the tax—and cashing in on it. Hutchinson's family were not the only consignees for tea in Boston; Richard Clarke, one of his wealthy relatives, would also prosper.

# RICHARD CLARKE: "ENEMY OF THE PEOPLE"

Richard Clarke barely had more going for him in the eyes of Bostonians than Thomas Hutchinson. Problematically for Clarke, he was related to Hutchinson—another example of the breeding that happened among rich Boston families. After graduating from Harvard, Clarke became a merchant, and by the 1770s, Richard Clarke and Sons was one the largest importers of tea in Massachusetts. His office at the end of Long Wharf on King Street was prime real estate, as was his large home on School Street. He was well known in Boston as a man of means. His wife, Elizabeth Winslow, gave birth to twelve children, and one of their daughters,

Self-portrait of John Singleton Copley. *National Portrait Gallery, Smithsonian Institution.*

Susannah, married quite well (if not financially, but for posterity). In 1769, she accepted the proposal of John Singleton Copley, arguably the finest portrait artist in Boston.

Clarke's political and economic standing in Boston made him and his sons the perfect candidates to be named consignees of the British East India Company tea. Like the Stamp Act nearly a decade before, such a commission was given only to the elite members of society, including the Clarkes and Hutchinsons. And just like with Oliver and the Stamp Act, Clarke would learn that this new position placed his family in danger. But unlike Andrew Oliver, who resigned as Stamp Act collector after the mob intimidated him, Clarke and his sons would not back down as easily. Clarke was a brave, headstrong man who had stood up to Bostonians a few years before. He had not complied with the nonimportation agreement of 1769, even after repeatedly being named an enemy to the country in a newspaper. He wore the moniker of "enemy" well. He made his money how he needed to and remained steadfastly loyal to the Crown, even if subjected to intimidation, as he would be when news broke of the Tea Act and his family's role in enforcing it.

Richard Clarke was awakened by a loud knock on the front door of his home in the early morning hours of November 2, 1773. He looked outside and saw two shadowy men in his garden. They brought a note for him, which instructed Clarke to appear at the Liberty Tree at noon the following day to resign his post as tea consignee. Hutchinson's sons had received a similar note earlier that same night. Clarke must have laughed at this pathetic attempt to intimidate him. The next day, as the rebels should have expected, Clarke didn't show at the Liberty Tree. He may have been stubborn, but he wasn't stupid. He knew only trouble awaited him and his sons at the so-called Liberty Tree. John Hancock, Joseph Warren and Samuel Adams lamely stood around waiting for an hour, along with a crowd of nearly five hundred people. And still, Clarke was a no-show. He had stood up Boston's most influential rebels, reminding them that they had less power than they thought. They'd have to do more than send a mean note to get his attention.

Annoyed by Clarke's truancy, a group of eight or nine rebels, including local street tough William Molineux and fervent rebel Benjamin Church, marched from the Liberty Tree to King Street. They headed straight to Clarke's warehouse, where Clarke and some of Boston's elites were in his office talking about this latest drama. The rebels walked in and told Clarke that he had insulted the people by not showing up at the Liberty Tree. You can imagine how little Clarke cared about hurting rebels' feelings. Molineux asked Clarke to agree not to import the East India Company tea and send back any tea that arrived in Boston. True to Clarke's character, he refused in a "haughty manner." Stunned by the refusal, Molineux did what he did best: he threatened Clarke with the wrath of Bostonians because Clarke and his sons would now (once again) be considered "enemies of the people."[70]

While the two sides were bickering inside Clarke's office, a crowd gathered out front. After getting nowhere with Clarke, Molineux walked outside and announced to the people that Clarke would not stop the importation of tea. Hearing of his refusal, the mob ran toward Clarke's store. A few of Clarke's employees rushed to try to lock the door, but it did no good. The crowd ripped the door from its hinges and tried to proceed upstairs. The angry mob was blocked by nearly twenty employees from proceeding up the staircase, due to the good fortune of the narrow staircase not being able to hold a crowd of people. This led to a standoff (which, for a mob, is the most boring way an attack could go). After about an hour and a half, the crowd wandered off. Clarke had drawn a line—the rebels could not physically or emotionally intimidate him. And that, of course, angered the mob. One newspaper reported that after this encounter, some men "who felt personal courage and bodily strength" wanted to take on the Clarkes, determined they could best them. These toughs called for "a real trial of their mettle arm to arm." Be careful what you wish for. Within two weeks, the Clarkes would further show that they weren't just pampered, privileged members of Boston's elites. They were street, too.[71]

The issue with the Clarkes came to a head on November 17, when one of Hancock's ships brought news to Boston that a ship filled with East India Company tea had left London for Boston. With the threat of the tea now more real, a mob got busy. Men went to Thomas Hutchinson's house to tell his sons that they could not accept the tea when it arrived. No one was home, so the crowd headed to the Clarke residence. Hutchinson claimed "their number as they were passing greatly increased," as people were eager to jump in on the action. The Clarkes had family and friends over that night and were disrupted around eight o'clock that evening by a violent knock at the

Portrait by John Singleton Copley of his family. Richard Clarke, Copley's father-in-law, sits in front of Copley, and Clarke's daughter, Susannah, is to the right. *National Gallery of Art.*

door. The Clarkes and their guests heard shouting and horns blowing from one to two hundred angry men in the Clarkes' garden. The women were ushered upstairs to safety while the men attempted to block the entrances. Those trapped inside likely recalled the destruction of the homes of Oliver and Hutchinson, who fortunately weren't home at the time of those attacks. It wasn't yet known what a Boston mob would do to a royal official if he was inside a home they targeted. It turned out the mob needed to be more afraid of the men inside than the Clarkes needed to fear the mob.[72]

As the mob tried to force open the house's locked door, one of Richard Clarke's sons went upstairs. He hung his head out of the window and shouted at the crowd to disperse. The crowd responded "with double violence" by throwing stones at him and the house. The desperate man either came unhinged or used the mob's behavior as an excuse to frighten the people who'd been tormenting his family. He grabbed a pistol and shot into the crowd. Luckily, no one was injured, but such brazenness incited a new wave of objects thrown at the house, breaking the home's windows and damaging some of the Clarkes' furniture. Attempting to calm the crowd before the fracas became deadly, some of the mob's leaders reminded the participants that there was a town meeting scheduled for the next morning. There, in a more proper forum, they could once again try to force the Clarkes' hands, as well as those of other consignees. The crowd eventually dispersed. Richard Clarke and Sons had shown themselves to be formidable opponents.[73]

## THE COUNTDOWN BEGINS

On November 28, 1773, the first ship filled with East India Company tea, *Dartmouth*, docked in Boston Harbor. With its arrival, a countdown began. Once a ship docked, British law required that its cargo be unloaded within twenty days and the required taxes paid. If that didn't happen, customs officials could seize the cargo, where it and the ship would be sold at auction. The rebels had twenty short days to figure out what to do with the tea. Rebel leaders, including members of the North End Caucus, met at one of their favorite spots, the Green Dragon Tavern, to discuss how to deal with the tea and the consignees.

The illustrious Green Dragon Tavern. Its dragon sign is visible above the door, and the symbol in the left corner is a nod to the Masonic lodge on its top floor. *Courtesy of the American Antiquarian Society.*

Faneuil Hall in the eighteenth century, located in the center of Dock Square. The building was much smaller then than it is today. *Library of Congress.*

A larger group of Massachusetts residents met at Faneuil Hall on Monday, November 29. All of the heavy hitters were there: Samuel Adams, John Hancock, Joseph Warren, William Molineux and Benjamin Church. As Faneuil Hall became too crowded, they moved over to the Old South Meeting House on Cornhill Street, now Washington Street. Old South Meeting House was the largest building in Boston in the eighteenth century, so it was an ideal location for the larger crowds. The rebels decided the tea must be sent back to London immediately. The person they thought was best to target was Francis Rotch, the owner of *Dartmouth*. The group demanded that Rotch send the tea back to London. He said he couldn't do that without a pass from the governor, none other than Thomas Hutchinson. Over the next two weeks, rebel leaders and committees continued to pester Rotch and the consignees to send the tea back or have Hutchinson grant the ships the right to leave. The desperate situation was compounded when two more ships carrying East India Company tea, *Beaver* and *Eleanor*, arrived in Boston Harbor.

Adding to their headache and ineffectual tactics against the Tea Act so far, Boston's rebels felt external pressure to act tough in this situation. New York and Philadelphia—which had already intimidated their tea agents into resigning—were dubious about Boston's commitment to resist the Tea Act after bailing on the nonimportation agreement a few years before. A taunt from Philadelphia was printed in the *Boston Gazette* on December 13, 1773. It read, "Our Tea Consignees have all resign'd, and you need not fear; the Tea will not be landed here or at New-York. All that we fear is, that you will shrink at Boston." It continued, "You have fail'd us in the Importation of Tea from London since the Non-importation Agreement, and we fear you will suffer this to be landed." Philadelphia had thrown down a gauntlet. Boston better not shrink. Meanwhile, the clock was ticking. With every day that passed, colonists were getting closer to the twenty-day deadline, December 17, and nowhere closer to a resolution.[74]

On December 16, the day before Boston's deadline to unload the tea, a crowd gathered at the Old South Meeting House. It was a cold and rainy day, but it didn't stop nearly five thousand people, by Samuel Adams's estimation, from making the trip and cramming themselves into the meetinghouse. It was not just people from Boston who came—people from the surrounding countryside also arrived in droves. They were sitting around and waiting for the arrival of one man, Rotch. He had agreed to travel to Hutchinson's country house in Milton, Massachusetts, and ask one final time for the governor's permission for *Dartmouth* to leave the harbor. From a safe distance in the suburbs, however, Hutchinson refused. Rotch brought word back to the Old South Meeting House around 6:00 p.m. that Hutchinson had denied the request. After a slow-moving morning and afternoon, the crowd was finally going to have some action.[75]

Samuel Adams stood to make a pivotal speech. As he proclaimed that "this meeting can do no more to save the country," whoops from outside and cries of "Rally Mohawks!" were heard. These were signals for rebels to head down to the harbor. The crowd inside began shouting, "Boston Harbor—a tea pot tonight!" and "a number of people huzza'd in the Street." It was a lively and festive crowd. The crowd's excitement grew as many of them headed out of Old South Meeting House and down Milk Street, before turning toward the waterfront. They reached Griffin's Wharf where the three ships were docked. Rebels were about to throw a new kind of party.[76]

# DESTRUCTION OF THE TEA

Only about 20 to 30 men had been invited to participate in the destruction of the tea, as the Boston Tea Party was called at that time. They were young, working-class men who were not well known in town. Adams, Hancock and

Warren, for example, posed too big a risk to participate. Some men who got caught up in the moment joined as well, bringing the total number of participants to about 150 men. For the participants whose ages are known, more than a third of them were under the age of twenty-one. One twenty-two-year-old participant, Sammy Gore, clearly didn't allow his injured left hand from Ebenezer Richardson's shooting in 1770 to stop him from participating. It likely motivated him all the more. Alongside Sammy Gore was one of his fellow Freemasons, silversmith Paul Revere.[77]

The tea party differed from previous mob violence in Boston because the mob was not set on rampant, uncontrollable violence. The destruction of the tea, rather, was a highly orchestrated affair. The participants were orderly and assigned into one of three groups, each of which would board a ship. The men spent the next two to three hours using their tomahawks or hatchets to smash open 342 chests of tea—totaling forty-six tons—before tossing them overboard. This wasn't easy work, either. The full-sized chests weighed approximately four hundred pounds. Splintering the chests was essential to the tea sinking, but dumping it overboard didn't ensure the tea would actually float away. Humorously, the tide was low that night, and some of the tea leaves simply gathered in the muddy area surrounding the ships. Some young boys went down to the mudflats and attempted to spread the tea with their hands and feet. When high tide came, the tea and chests were finally swept off.

A lot is made in popular memory of the participants disguising themselves as Native Americans. Like many historical myths, there is some truth here, but it is not wholly accurate. The men who had been invited to participate in the destruction of the tea had fairly complete Native American disguises. But the men who spontaneously joined in had not prepared elaborate disguises. They improvised by covering their faces with soot, grease and lamp black. Some simply draped themselves in blankets. It also wasn't a covert affair, as may be imagined. There were between one and two thousand people who watched the unloading of the tea. It wasn't just curious Bostonians who were seeing the event unfold. The British and their warships were also keeping a very close eye on the ships from the harbor. The soldiers could not fire or intervene without an order from the governor or his council, so they could do nothing more than watch (and likely stew with contempt for the rebels). After the tea was dumped and there was nothing left to see or do, the participants and spectators straggled home, and a calm settled over Boston the next day. As could be expected, Boston didn't stay calm for long.

# THE DESTRUCTION CONTINUES

There was over a foot of snow in Boston in late January. Young boys made the most of it on January 25, 1774. They were sledding down Copp's Hill, the high point of the North End. An unpopular customs officer—so unpopular he had been tarred and feathered in New Hampshire the previous year—John Malcom, did not seem to be enjoying the snow and yelled at a young boy whose sled smashed into him. A bystander, George Hewes, who had participated in the tea party six weeks earlier, walked by and chided Malcom for yelling at the boy. Malcom raised his cane and struck Hewes in the head, leaving him unconscious and with a deep, two-inch cut.

An avuncular and aged George Hewes, decades after being struck by Malcom. *The Miriam and Ira D. Wallach Division of Art, Prints and Photographs: Print Collection, New York Public Library.*

Word about the attack on Hewes quickly spread in Boston, and by eight o'clock that night, Boston's toughest thugs descended on Malcom's house and surrounded it. He and his family scurried to the second floor and hid, but not before Malcom stuck his sword out of a broken window and made minor contact with someone. That would be the only shot he'd get in all night. Men with axes climbed toward the second floor where Malcom and his family were trapped inside. The Malcoms would have heard their windows shatter and then seen the mob enter their home. Fortunately, the mob had the decency to not physically harm his family, although we can say nothing of the psychological harm they endured as the head of their household was hoisted out of the window and down to the ground. Malcom was then tied up. Stripped down. Warm tar was poured on his body, and before the tar could dry, he was covered in feathers. Boston's weather in January meant the tar would quickly harden. Malcom was then dumped into a cart in which he would become the grand marshal of a most embarrassing parade.

The mob first took Malcom up King Street, the center of town, and stopped in front of the Old State House before heading over to the edge of town, Boston Neck, where the hangings took place. The men put a noose around Malcom's neck and threatened to hang him. They also tied him up, beat him and whipped him "with great Barbarity," as several people watched. He then was dumped back into the cart, and for a couple more hours, he was paraded through Boston. At some point, Malcom became unconscious. The mob eventually dropped him back at his house around midnight. It would be the most brutal tarring and feathering to take place in all of colonial America. Malcom miraculously survived the event, even going back to London with pieces of his own skin that had flaked off as proof of his horrid treatment.[78]

Boston's destructive streak didn't stop with the Boston Tea Party or the tarring and feathering of Malcom. The rebels were on a roll, even hosting a second tea party. On March 6, a ship arrived in Boston Harbor carrying thirty chests of tea. The following day, about sixty men went down to the harbor dressed as Native Americans, forced the ship's crew below deck and dumped the tea overboard. Sixty men was far more than was necessary to take care of thirty chests of tea, but rebels were going to great lengths to show that they were in charge and would continue to resist taxation. And now was the time to do it. The rebels were enjoying the golden hour between Parliament hearing about the first tea party and sending word back about their punishment. It took six weeks for news to reach London and about eight weeks to return home. That timing also didn't account for Parliament legislating, so the rebels had plenty of time to continue their mobbing, as Malcom and the crew of the ship subjected to the second tea party knew too well.

## COERCING THE COLONIES

Parliament determined that the punishment for the Boston Tea Party needed to finally extinguish Boston's rebellious spirit and firmly establish parliamentary control. It passed a series of laws, known as the Coercive Acts, on a rolling basis, which meant that Boston's surprise and annoyance would crop up all summer. The Boston Port Bill was the first law passed, and it shut down Boston's harbor beginning in June 1774. The harbor would not reopen until Bostonians paid for the tea destroyed, which was over $1 million in today's value. As a maritime economy and society, this act was intended to cripple Boston, and it did just that almost immediately after going into effect. In response, the Boston Committee of Correspondence requested help from other towns. It wrote to Philadelphia that the Boston Port Bill left the town without a "Means of Subsistence as to keep us from perishing with

Cold and Hunger." Donations from other Massachusetts towns and colonies began pouring in, having to arrive in Salem first because they could not be processed in Boston's closed harbor.[79]

No act(s) to date did more to turn colonial backs on the British government than the Coercive Acts, with each of them seeming more egregious than the last. After the Boston Port Bill came the Massachusetts Government Act. It altered the charter of Massachusetts and shut down popular elections for all government posts. All members of the Governor's Council were now going to be appointed by the royal government instead of the House of Representatives. Judges could be removed without the council's consent and be replaced by the governor. In one fell swoop, the Massachusetts Government Act wiped out any government by the people, something Massachusetts residents had been proud of for nearly a century and a half.

More acts followed that increased British power. The Administration of Justice Act was a temporary order to last three years and allowed any civil or military official on trial for a capital offense in Massachusetts to be tried in England. It only took a request from the governor to make that happen. Colonists referred to this as the Murder Act because they believed any official who went back to England for his trial would surely be acquitted. The Quartering Act of 1774 empowered British officers and royal officials to seize uninhabited buildings if necessary to quarter soldiers but still did not allow for soldiers to stay in private homes. The final law was the Quebec Act, which permitted Catholics freedom of worship and extended Quebec as far as the Ohio River to the south and Mississippi River on the west. This act irked both northern and southern colonies. Massachusetts was filled with staunch Congregationalists, whose history was steeped in stifling others' religious freedoms—especially those of Catholics—so they didn't want to grant them freedom of worship. Southern colonists objected to the Quebec Act because it stopped them from being able to speculate the land north of the Ohio River. With this final Coercive Act, Parliament had done a spectacular job of punishing Boston and all of Massachusetts for a handful of residents' involvement in the tea party. Its extreme measures also alienated the other colonies. Gage wrote, "Nobody here or at home could have conceived, that the Acts made for the Massachusett's Bay, could have created such a Ferment throughout the Continent, and united the whole in one Common Cause." The colonies uniting around Boston would be a problem for Gage because he had been tasked with administering and enforcing the Coercive Acts.[80]

General Thomas Gage had spent nearly three decades in the army and was commander in chief of the British troops occupying North America, so he was considered the perfect man to bring Boston to its knees. Lord Dartmouth, who had replaced Lord Hillsborough in 1772 as secretary of state of American affairs, recalled Hutchinson from his post as governor. Dartmouth explained that "General Gage's continuance in the government will most probably not be of long duration." He indicated that once Gage restored order to Massachusetts, the king would likely reinstate Hutchinson as governor. In early 1774, Hutchinson sailed for London for what he thought would be a temporary stay, while Gage confidently arrived in Boston with two thousand troops, believing that would be enough to enforce the Coercive Acts. Both Hutchinson and Gage would be let down.[81]

General Thomas Gage, whose unassuming portrait echoes much of his rule in North America. *The Miriam and Ira D. Wallach Division of Art, Prints and Photographs: Print Collection, New York Public Library.*

## A "COMMON CAUSE"

Gage needed a plan to shut down the rebellion. It was simple. Gage believed that if he could get his hands on colonists' ammunition, he would stop Massachusetts's ability to violently rebel. For generations, Americans received their gunpowder from Great Britain, but in the fall of 1774, after increasing tensions, the British cut off their gunpowder exports to Massachusetts. Gunpowder was a challenging item to create, requiring peter, a resource not easily or efficiently produced in the colonies. Without fresh supplies arriving, colonists needed to safeguard their limited supply of gunpowder, which was often stored in a centrally located magazine. Gage was going to take the colonists' gunpowder back. His first target was Cambridge.

As Gage was plotting, Samuel Adams was fuming. He wrote to men in other colonies, asking them to help Boston in opposing the Coercive Acts. Christopher Gadsden in South Carolina received a letter, which included some of the most overt and poetic calls to unity. Adams wrote, "The British

Colonists in North America are an inseparable Band of Brothers, each of whom resents an Attack upon the Rights of one as an Attack upon the Rights of all." He asked his old friend in Virginia, Richard Henry Lee, to consider Boston as "suffering in the common Cause," and requested that Virginia "support them in the Conflict." Virginia was sufficiently alarmed by the Coercive Acts that it proposed a meeting of all of the colonies to discuss the Coercive Acts and the increasingly tense relationship with Great Britain. This meeting would become the First Continental Congress. Finally, Boston might receive some political support from other colonies.[82]

The First Continental Congress convened in Philadelphia on September 5, 1774. Philadelphia was a natural meeting space for several reasons. First, it wasn't Boston, the center of trouble. Second, it was fairly central to most colonies throughout North America. And finally, it was the largest of all towns in America. Massachusetts sent four delegates: Samuel Adams, John Adams, Robert Treat Paine and Thomas Cushing. They couldn't travel by sea—the fastest mode of transport—because Boston Harbor was shut down, so they set off in Cushing's coach. Traveling by coach, even the most glamorous, wasn't an easy ride, with dusty and bumpy roads. The delegates, however, left behind an even bumpier situation in Boston. Just before the Continental Congress began, Gage would enact his plan to seize gunpowder. It wouldn't go as he planned and would cause four thousand armed men to gather outside of Boston, all ready to take on the British.

## FROM PAST TO PRESENT

### GREEN DRAGON TAVERN

*The Green Dragon was a large and lively tavern on Union Street and a frequent meeting place for the Sons of Liberty. It derived its name from the large copper dragon sculpture that protruded out from the front of the building. In the salty air, the copper oxidized, and the dragon turned green. It "had a curled tail; and from its mouth projected a fearful looking tongue, the wonder of all the boys who dwelt in the neighborhood." The building had a tavern downstairs, and the second floor housed St. Andrew's Masonic Lodge (where Revere, Hancock* and Warren were members). Today, if you go to the Green Dragon, you'll be visiting the tavern in name alone, although it is not far from the original location, which is now a subway station. The Green Dragon has local craft beers on draft and a congenial staff.[83]

The exterior of the Green Dragon Tavern today. *Photograph by the author.*

## Old South Meeting House

*Old South Meeting House was built in 1729 as a Puritan place of worship. It was the largest building in Boston at this time and could be used for town meetings if Faneuil Hall became too crowded. In the 1870s, Old South Meeting House was going to be demolished before a preservation group rallied to keep and restore it—one of the first efforts of its kind. The building is currently a museum on the Freedom Trail. When you visit, look upward from the pews to the rafters and imagine the place packed to the gills with impatient Bostonians wanting to hear news from Francis Rotch about the tea*

Old South Meeting House on Washington Street. *Courtesy of Ryan Shelby.*

*languishing in the harbor. And then imagine the war whoops outside calling you down to Griffin's Wharf.*

## SITE OF THE BOSTON TEA PARTY

There is some dispute about where Griffin's Wharf is located today, but there's no dispute that it is currently occupied by a city street. The waterfront, including the markers for eighteenth-century wharves, were filled in in the nineteenth century. Griffin's Wharf—and the site of the Boston Tea Party—was likely somewhere on Atlantic Avenue today near Pearl Street. The Boston Tea Party Ships and Museum is a short walk from that location.

# 6

# Confrontation and Chaos in the Countryside

*Key Player: Paul Revere, the Spirited Messenger*

It must have been awkward in the beginning. Most of the men had never heard of one another, much less met one another. They might have run into one another at one of Philadelphia's taverns beforehand, but many would meet for the first time at the small building where they'd be crammed together for the next few weeks. The delegates from twelve colonies—Georgia didn't attend—gathered at Carpenter's Hall, a small two-story building, for the First Continental Congress. Given the hall's small size, it is hard to imagine fifty-four men comfortably standing in this building, never mind sitting down at desks or writing tables. And it wasn't likely to be a completely harmonious meeting. The representatives from Massachusetts knew that many delegates cast a wary (and weary) eye their way, since they came from the matrix of rebellion. And the men from Massachusetts did nothing to dampen such views. The Congress hadn't been meeting two full days before a serious issue with Massachusetts needed to be addressed. Redcoats had shot and killed some peaceful colonists in Cambridge, a few miles from Boston.

Or so the rumors said. It took three days for the Continental Congress to learn the truth, which was that, on September 1, 1774, about three hundred soldiers marched to a powder house in Cambridge, stole some gunpowder and brought it back to Castle Island. It was a quiet and nonviolent seizure and fulfilled Gage's goal to take colonial powder. No shots had been fired, and no one had been killed. But when word of the powder raid spread to the countryside, so did a rumor that the local militia had tried to stop the redcoats from stealing the powder, and in response, the British soldiers shot

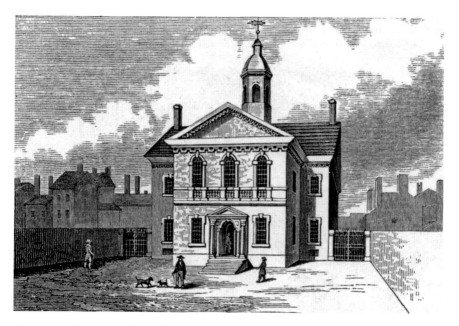

The modest Carpenter's Hall in Philadelphia, where the First Continental Congress was held in 1774. *The Miriam and Ira D. Wallach Division of Art, Prints and Photographs: Print Collection, New York Public Library.*

and killed six colonists. Hearing this, nearly four thousand men grabbed their guns and gathered on Cambridge Common the following day, Friday, September 2, ready to take on the British soldiers. When the crowd learned that nobody had been killed, they still used their considerable manpower to successfully demand that newly appointed members of the Governor's Council (thank you, Government Act) from Cambridge resign. Meanwhile, men from towns twenty to thirty miles away continued to mobilize that morning, with estimates as high as twenty thousand men marching toward Cambridge. This confrontation became known as the Powder Alarm, and it (oddly enough) would be Gage's most successful powder raid.

In Philadelphia, not all of the delegates were relieved to learn that the redcoats hadn't actually fired on colonists. It's not that they wanted Massachusetts men dead, but the delegates had been quite alarmed by the story and now thought that the false rumors reflected poorly on Massachusetts. Joseph Galloway, from conservative Pennsylvania, cynically believed that the Powder Alarm was simply part of a plan concocted by Samuel Adams and the Massachusetts radicals to goad the other colonies into their fight against the British. It would not be the last time that other colonies accused Massachusetts of projecting its problems onto everyone else. It was easy to see why they felt that way when Massachusetts (yet again) demanded the Congress's attention a short time after learning the truth about the Powder Alarm.

# "SPIRITED AND PATRIOTICK RESOLVES"

Back in Massachusetts, Joseph Warren was busy leading meetings to discuss the Coercive Acts. The Government Act banned any town meetings in Massachusetts, but rebels cleverly got around that by holding county meetings. The meetings of Suffolk County, where Boston was located, were led by Warren. At one of these meetings, Warren presented the attendees with a document he wrote, aptly named the Suffolk Resolves, which contained nineteen resolves he had collated from Suffolk's past meetings. The Resolves were written with two audiences in mind: General Gage and the Continental Congress. In them, the rebels of Suffolk County rejected the Coercive Acts and laid out their plans to oppose them. First, all colonies were going to boycott British imports. Second, because Gage had dismissed the General Court in the summer of 1774, they were going to establish a Provincial Congress—Government Act be damned—to fill in as the temporary local government. Finally, Massachusetts would raise its militia and start preparing militarily for a potential confrontation. A day after their approval in Massachusetts, Paul Revere set off with the Resolves to Philadelphia, traveling with urgency.

The Suffolk Resolves were the boldest and most radical of all of colonial actions to date, which made sense since they were in response to the most radical actions by Parliament to date. Samuel Adams was pleased with Warren's work, referring to the document as "the spirited and patriotick Resolves." He was confident that "America will make a point of supporting Boston to the utmost," even if Boston was trying to establish an unprecedented rival government to Gage's. Adams arranged to have the Suffolk Resolves read aloud in the Continental Congress. On September 17, the Resolves were read paragraph by paragraph, with each one unanimously approved by the delegates. It was monumental that the delegates agreed on an issue, and one that involved Massachusetts, no less. On September 24, Revere was sent express back to Boston to let them know that the Suffolk Resolves had been unanimously approved by the Continental Congress.[84]

# CLOSE CALLS

In the fall of 1774 and the winter of 1775, in and around Boston, there seemed to be a dangerous and increased pattern of close calls between redcoats and colonists. It began with the Powder Alarm in September and continued in February and March. Despite his first powder raid ending with trouble, Gage still seemed to believe the best course of action was to steal colonial powder and munitions. To avoid the problems he encountered in Cambridge, Gage was determined to keep his next raid, targeting Salem, a secret. (He wouldn't.) The townspeople of Salem had learned about his plan and moved their munitions before the troops arrived. Not knowing he was on a doomed mission, Lieutenant Colonel Alexander Leslie led 250 redcoats to Salem on February 26, 1775. Gage had ordered Leslie to seize Salem's cannons, but he and his men could not get across the river to access them because the townspeople had pulled up the drawbridge. (The cannons weren't there anyway.) The redcoats stood by the river as people from Salem gathered to taunt and insult the soldiers. Growing frantic, Leslie met with local leaders to discuss how to retreat with a little bit of dignity. Mercifully for Leslie, they cut him some slack. They agreed to put down the drawbridge, allow Leslie and his troops to pass over the river, have a cursory look and then turn around and go straight back to Boston. It was a humiliating misadventure for Leslie and the redcoats.

It was also a disastrous outcome for General Gage. He hadn't been able to get the munitions, and worse, the Salem powder raid taught more colonists in Massachusetts that they could get the best of the British army. For the past ten years, the rebels had grown increasingly bold in the face of British policies, people and military tactics that they didn't support. Gage knew the situation was bad, but he didn't let on to Lord Dartmouth what a train wreck it had been. He wrote, being completely literal, that the people in Salem "assembled in great Numbers with Threats and abuse, but the Colonel pursued his Orders." Yes, Colonel Leslie "pursued his orders," but only because the men in Salem had allowed him to.[85]

Hostilities heated up in Boston a week after the Salem powder raid. Ever since 1766, Bostonians celebrated several anniversaries on the resistance calendar, including the ransacking of Hutchinson's home, the repeal of the Stamp Act and the Boston Massacre. March 5, 1775, was a Sunday, so the Boston Massacre anniversary was moved to March 6. Thousands of people gathered at the Old South Meeting House around ten o'clock in the morning and saw the pulpit covered in a somber black cloth. Forty British officers also walked in, crowding in toward the front. Samuel Adams claimed that he took great care of the officers by "inviting them into convenient Seats." The officers now sat dangerously close to the heavy hitters of the rebel movement, including Adams, Hancock and Dr. Benjamin Church. Joseph Warren, dressed in a toga, went to the podium and spoke melodramatically about the men who died in the massacre. (He went so far as to mention the tragedy of the orphans left behind because their fathers had been killed, even though none of the Boston Massacre victims had children.) After Warren stepped down, Samuel Adams went to the pulpit. He called for the people to mourn the "bloody massacre" of 1770. The word massacre set off the British soldiers. The redcoats hissed at Adams and protested, shouting, "Oh fie!" In the tense and crowded room, people thought the British soldiers were shouting, "Fire!" The attendees panicked and pushed toward the doors and jumped out of the windows, thinking the building would soon be engulfed in flames.[86]

Just as people were escaping Old South Meeting House, a regiment of British soldiers marched by with fifes playing and drums beating. Many townspeople fleeing the meetinghouse thought they were about to be attacked. It was an uneasy few moments before Bostonians realized that there was no fire and that the redcoats were only drilling. Samuel Adams claimed that "were it not for the Danger of precipitating a Crisis, not a Man of them would have been spared." The atmosphere in Boston was incendiary—it seemed violence could erupt at any moment.[87]

## GAGE CONTINUES TO PLOT, BUT SO DOES PAUL REVERE

In March 1775, the Provincial Congress—established by the Suffolk Resolves—began meeting in Concord. John Hancock and Samuel Adams traveled to the countryside together to be closer to the meetings. They stayed at the Hancock-Clarke parsonage in Lexington with Hancock's cousin Lucy and her husband, Jonas Clarke—no relation to merchant Richard Clarke. Hancock was president of the Congress, and he and Adams commuted from Lexington to Concord for the meetings, about five miles away. When the Provincial Congress adjourned in April, Hancock and Adams decided not to return to Boston. There was talk that Gage planned to arrest both of them, so they waited in Lexington until they had to leave for Philadelphia for the Second Continental Congress.

The talk about Hancock and Adams being arrested had some merit. On April 14, 1775, Gage received orders from Lord Dartmouth instructing him to finally and firmly take action to stop the rebellion in Massachusetts. "Arrest the principal actors and abettors in the Provincial Congress," if necessary, wrote Dartmouth, but put an end to this. Gage decided not to heed Dartmouth's suggestion to arrest rebel leaders but instead continue his ill-fated plans to steal colonial munitions and powder. His next target was Concord, about twenty miles from Boston. Concord was an ideal place to store munitions because it served as a crossroads between Boston and many towns west and north. The redcoats were to march there, destroy the stores and return home. What could be simpler?[88]

Despite his attempts to keep the plan a secret, Gage's cover was blown, yet again. On Tuesday evening, April 18, Bostonians saw redcoats gather at the base of Boston Common and alerted Joseph Warren, who was one of the only remaining rebel leaders in Boston. Warren summoned Paul Revere to his house in the North End and told him that people had seen soldiers, "composed of Light troops, and Grenadiers, marching to the bottom of the Common." They were going to take a sea route—the Charles River—to Lexington. He told Revere to "go to Lexington, and inform Mr. Samuel Adams, and the Hon[orable] John Hancock." He was also to alert Concord, a town five miles from Lexington, that the British might also head there too and "destroy the Colony stores." Warren mistakenly believed that Gage's plan included arresting Hancock and Adams, so Revere's primary goal that night was to alert them.[89]

Warren chose Revere to be his messenger because he was a trusted rebel with plenty of street credibility. The child of a French Huguenot father and a British mother, Paul Revere was born in the North End to a comfortable family. His dad was a silversmith, who arrived to North America with the poetic name Apollos Rivoire, which he anglicized to Paul Revere. Life in Boston at this time put Revere's father in proximity to two other apprentices honing their crafts and whose prominence would grow: Thomas Hancock, who later would become the richest man in Boston and adoptive father to John Hancock, and Benjamin Franklin, who tinkered in a few trades before finding that publishing suited him perfectly. Paul apprenticed with his father until he was old enough to operate his own shop.

Paul carried on his father's trade and became one of the finest silversmiths in the North American colonies. His work came with a bonus: it gave him

John Singleton Copley's 1768 portrait of Paul Revere. Copley didn't typically paint artisans, but he portrays Revere as a talented and thoughtful silversmith. *Museum of Fine Arts, Boston.*

unique access to both the lower orders of men and the rebel leaders in Boston. As an artisan, Revere could relate to and mingle easily among the lower sorts in Boston, who were often the ones joining violent mobs. The wealthy wanted what Revere crafted and frequently commissioned his works of silver for their homes, including teapots, bowls and cutlery, so they were familiar with him, too. Revere also loved the tavern culture that was so prevalent in Boston at this time, which further drew him into many political circles. He lived a short walk to one of his favorite taverns, the Green Dragon Tavern. Revere would go to the taverns and see "what was acting," a phrase he used to find out news. In his early adulthood he joined the Masons, which expanded his network and contact with influential political thinkers, including Warren and Hancock.

Because Revere was so connected, he made a perfect messenger, and rebels often used him to transmit information. Just two days before his most famous ride, Warren had sent Revere to Lexington to warn Adams and Hancock that an actionable warning might be coming soon. On his way back home, Revere stopped in Charlestown and devised a plan with some of the men there. He figured that when the actual alarm was sounded, Gage would block off any exit points in Boston to prevent express riders. Revere anticipated "it would be difficult to Cross the Charles River, or git over the Boston neck." They devised a way to covertly alert Charlestown, in case a rider would need to leave from there. Christ Church in the City of Boston—known today as Old North Church—had the highest steeple in Boston at 191 feet. It was easily seen from Charlestown, making it the ideal spot to send a signal. Revere recalled that they agreed "if the British went out by Water, we should shew two Lanthorns in the North Church Steeple; and if by Land, one, as a Signal."[90]

View today of Old North Church's steeple from Charlestown. As the tallest point in Boston at that time, it was an ideal place to send a signal across the harbor. *Courtesy of Ryan Shelby.*

After being summoned by Warren on the night of April 18, Revere went to John Pulling and Robert Newman and instructed them to hang two lanterns in Old North's belfry. The lights were only up for a moment—likely a few seconds—but long enough for the people in Charlestown to receive the signal and get a horse ready for Revere. He then rowed across the Charles River to Charlestown and told them "what was acting," as they fetched his horse. Warren also sent out another rider that night, William Dawes, who would take the longer route over the Neck. Revere was too well known in Boston to be waved through Gage's barricades, but Dawes disguised himself as a man from the countryside and passed through. Dawes's land route was approximately twenty-one miles to Lexington, while Revere rowing to Charlestown cut his route down to about sixteen miles.[91]

## SOUNDING THE ALARM

Revere began his ride at about eleven o'clock that "very pleasant" night on what he called "a very good Horse." Many aspects of this ride have been reduced to legend. We often imagine Revere shouting, "The British are coming! The British are coming!" This did not happen. Quite simply, all colonists were British at this time, so that warning wouldn't make sense. Instead, Revere exclaimed that "the regulars were coming out." Regulars was a term for the soldiers in the British standing army. Revere also didn't ride alone that night. Not only was Dawes a messenger, but riders were dispatched to more remote towns once their towns received the alarm. A town would also ring its church bells, which could be heard by a nearby town, which would then ring its church bells. The alarm quickly went viral, as more and more people spread the word.[92]

Revere made it to Lexington around midnight and told Hancock and Adams to flee. Revere had been there about a half an hour before Dawes arrived from the longer land route. Revere recalled that he and Dawes "refreshid our selves and set off for Concord." On their way, Revere and Dawes came across a doctor, Samuel Prescott, whom Revere knew to be a "high Son of Liberty." Prescott said that he would help them spread the alarm, claiming that he knew the people who lived between Lexington and Concord and could legitimize Revere and Dawes's message. Prescott was an excellent rider who was familiar with the terrain. It turned out to be a fortuitous meeting, for Prescott would be the only one of the three to make it to Concord.[93]

As they were riding, the three men came across British soldiers. Revere claimed they had their pistols out and shouted "[Goddamn] you stop. If you go an Inch further, you are a dead Man." Prescott then "jumped his Horse over a low Stone wall" and got away. Dawes also escaped and headed home shortly after, likely exhausted by all of the activity. Revere was not as lucky. He headed for a small, wooded area when six officers came upon him, "put their pistols to my Breast [and] ordered me to dismount." Revere said one officer "[c]lap'd his Pistol to my head and said he was going to ask me some questions." He threatened that if Revere did not tell the truth, "he would blow [my] brains out." Revere complied. The soldiers asked his name and what he was doing. He talked and talked, wanting to give Hancock and Adams enough time to leave Lexington. He even had the gall to warn the British troops that they would encounter trouble if they made it to Lexington. For some reason, the redcoats didn't shoot this mouthy and knowledgeable messenger. They released Revere and stole his borrowed horse. Revere headed back to Lexington for the second time that night.[94]

Revere returned to the Clarke house about three hours after he initially left and saw that Hancock and Adams were still there. Hancock's fiancée, Dolly, later recalled that when Revere first arrived, Hancock had taken

The Clarke-Hancock home, where John Hancock and Samuel Adams stayed. Revere arrived here to warn the rebel leaders to flee from Lexington. *Photograph by the author.*

out a sword and proclaimed that he would take on the redcoats. Adams shut Hancock down, telling him to leave the fighting to the men mustering outside. Revere urged them a second time to leave, and Hancock reluctantly acquiesced. Back in Boston, the redcoats weren't moving quickly either. They were led by Lieutenant Colonel Francis Smith—who did not have a gift for expediency—and Major John Pitcairn. Smith had his soldiers wait on Boston Common and in boats for two hours before sailing across the Charles River. When the troops finally landed in Cambridge, they did so in a swamp and dallied away at least another hour before moving out. This ensured that the soldiers' boots, not comfortable to begin with since they weren't designated for left or right feet, were soaked through as they waited (and waded) as the tide came in.

# THE "SHOT HEARD ROUND THE WORLD"

Based on Revere's alarm, about 130 men from Lexington's militia gathered on Lexington Common around one or two o'clock that morning. This represented 90 percent of the town's 144-man militia. The militia was mostly middle-aged, with some younger and older outliers, including a few men in their teens and a few in their fifties and sixties. Forty-six-year-old John Parker had been selected as the militia's leader because of his battle experience and clear head. And despite their ragtag appearance and lack of uniforms, many of the men on Lexington Common were battle-hardened soldiers who had been training together for generations and had recently fought in the French and Indian War. Most Massachusetts towns had their militia gather four times a year for training, but since the beginning of the year, Lexington and other towns had been training more earnestly in case there was armed conflict. These men mustered on the two-acre triangle-shaped Common and waited. Nothing happened in the first hour or so, and many men wandered home while others retired to Buckman Tavern, which bordered Lexington Common.

While the militia thought perhaps the regulars weren't coming out, Colonel Smith heard from roving redcoats that the countryside had been called to arms. "We found the country had intelligence or strong suspicion of our coming, had fired many signal guns and rung the alarm bells repeatedly," Smith recalled. He sent a messenger back to General Gage in Boston to tell him that reinforcements would be needed. The seven hundred British troops then continued toward Lexington with orders to take the men's weapons and disperse them. They were not to molest the soldiers or take any of them prisoners. The redcoats simply needed to get through Lexington to get to the munitions in Concord.[95]

As the British troops were getting closer to Lexington, only about seventy men from Lexington remained nearby. Parker had them line up in two feeble lines on the Common. The British troops arrived around dawn and lined themselves up within one hundred yards of the militia—seventy farmers versus seven hundred British soldiers. While Americans have been taught since a young age about what happens next, neither the redcoats nor the men from Lexington knew how this morning would unfold. Neither side would have anticipated that this standoff across a small town's public park would lead to a war or even to anyone being killed, as redcoats hadn't shot any colonists dead since the Boston Massacre.

Around the time the men were lining up, staring at one another and wondering what might happen next, Revere went to Buckman Tavern to retrieve a trunk of incriminating papers that Hancock had left behind. The trunk was large and heavy, measuring about two by four feet. Revere and another man hauled it out of the tavern and saw the column of "Ministeral Troops from the Chamber window" advancing. While carrying the trunk out to the woods to hide it, Revere passed by the militia gathered on Lexington Green. He heard Captain Parker say, "Let the troops pass by, and don't molest them." What Revere heard next would change the lives of every person in the colonies. It was the first shot of the Revolutionary War, later dubbed the "shot heard round the world." Revere recalled, "When one gun was fired, I…turned my head, and saw the smoake in front of the Troops…and then the whole fired." War had begun in Massachusetts.[96]

Historians don't know who fired the first shot, but they generally agree that the first shot came from behind the British—perhaps a gun that accidentally discharged, an overeager redcoat in the back of the columns or a spectator's desire for action. Just prior to it going off, the British officers had told the militia to lay down their arms. At the same time, Captain Parker told his men to hold their fire and disperse. Some militia had dispersed in a slow and disorderly way. But after the first shot was fired, the regulars began firing in earnest, despite not receiving orders to fire and ignoring their officers' orders to cease fire. The British officers could not get control of their men. It wasn't any less confusing for the militia, many of whom thought the regulars were firing blank warning shots. When the men from Lexington realized they were actually being hit and wounded, many ran.

The Battle of Lexington, as drawn shortly after the battle. The redcoats fire on the colonists from the center of Lexington Common while the militia flee in the bottom left and right corners. *Library of Congress.*

Only a few men stayed and were able to fire a few shots against the British. After several chaotic moments, Colonel Smith found a drummer, who beat orders for the redcoats to cease fire. The regulars stopped firing, and the battle was over.

The Battle of Lexington had been a terrifying display of the young, inexperienced British troops' lack of discipline and control. Worse, this bloodshed in Lexington had not been necessary to fulfill the redcoats' orders for that day. Gage had ordered them to capture and then destroy Concord's munitions, giving the soldiers very specific instructions to throw some items into a river and scatter musket balls on the road home. They were certainly not to shoot the colonists they encountered on the way. Given how the morning had gone, some officers thought that it was a terrible idea to continue with these orders. They were concerned that after the mission to Concord, they'd have to march back through Lexington on their way home to Boston. Smith pulled rank and told his men that these were their orders, and they were going to Concord to fulfill them.

Before the regulars departed from Lexington, they "fired a volley and gave three huzzas, by way of triumph and as expressive of the joy and victory

111

of the contest," according to Reverend Jonas Clarke. The British troops then marched toward Concord. As the redcoats departed and the smoke (literally) cleared, the townspeople of Lexington gathered on the common. They could still hear the British victory cheer ringing in their ears as they sadly counted eight men killed and seventeen men wounded. Most of the casualties had been shot in the back as they turned to run. No British soldier had been killed in the battle.[97] It would not be the last fight of the day for the men of Lexington.

# "CONTINUAL SKIRMISH FOR THE SPACE OF FIFTEEN MILES"

Luckily, Samuel Prescott had alerted Concord around 1:00 a.m. that the regulars were marching toward them. Concord's militia hid what was left of the munitions, although there wasn't much to hide because Revere's stop in Concord a few days earlier had prepared them. The Concord militia then went to the top of a hill past North Bridge and stared down at their village, unsure of how the morning would unfold. The regulars arrived in Concord around 8:00 a.m. and found a town that seemed to be deserted of men and munitions. The soldiers decided to split up. About half of them moved toward the edge of town, including some troops who guarded the North Bridge, cutting off the militia's access back to town. The other soldiers fulfilled their orders and seized any military stores they could find. Three cannons were confiscated, as were some gun carriages, entrenchment tools and musket balls. The balls were carelessly tossed into ponds (where they were later retrieved by the people of Concord) and what could be burned was made part of a bonfire. From the hillside, the militia—now comprising men from Concord, Lincoln, Carlisle, Bedford and Acton—could see smoke coming from the center of Concord and worried that the redcoats were trying to burn down Concord. They moved from their defensive position on the hill to an offensive position, coming within fifty yards of the regulars stationed at North Bridge.

The two groups stared at each other. The tension broke when, for the second time that morning, a redcoat fired without orders. More British soldiers fired. The militiamen were then told to fire, and they did not hesitate, hitting half of the British officers in their first volley. The redcoats were in a particularly vulnerable position because they were jumbled together at one end of the bridge, so they smartly retreated to the center of Concord. Without a game plan, the militia didn't follow the redcoats back into town. Neither side had anticipated firing shots, and neither knew what to do next. Stunned by the resolve that the militia had shown by squaring off against them at the bridge, the British officers decided that their men had seen enough action for the day and thought it best to cut their losses and head back to Boston.

The redcoats' retreat to Boston was going to be embattled. There was only one road leading toward Boston, and Gage claimed that "the whole Country" had assembled to make the march back a miserable one. Based on that morning's alarm, men from over forty towns west and north of Boston marched toward Concord, swelling colonial forces that afternoon to over 2,100 men. The militia then got busy. They concealed themselves along the road and fired on the redcoats, who were fairly easy targets with their conspicuous uniforms. Captain Parker and his men from Lexington—some bloodied and bandaged from the attack earlier that morning—got in some shots. They were concealed at the top of a hill, shot several men and even gave Colonel Smith a nasty thigh wound. This attack became known as Parker's Revenge. Smith described the militia's guerrilla warfare that day, saying, "They began to fire on us from behind the walls, ditches, trees etc."[98]

It wore on the regulars' nerves that they could not see who was attacking them. One officer sent out flankers to clear the houses ahead of his troops—and kill any snipers within—and they had some success. But the flankers grew less effective as the afternoon wore on. Gage reported that there was a "continual Skirmish for the Space of Fifteen Miles," as the troops tried to make their way back to Boston. When they were almost home, the redcoats marched to Charlestown instead, fearing an ambush in Boston. The regulars finally collapsed in the safety of Charlestown's highest hill, Bunker Hill, after being fired on for several hours and being on their feet for close to twenty hours.[99]

It had been a devastating day for the British army and General Gage, who was now three for three on botched powder raids. His troops acted hysterically and fired twice on British subjects without orders. And of the two battles that day—Lexington and Concord—the king's troops lost the deadlier one. Not only did they lose in Concord, but they were also severely beaten on the retreat home. According to Gage, the British had total casualties—dead, wounded, missing—of 272 men. In comparison, the colonists suffered only about one-third of that: 94 total casualties. The day after the battle, British general Hugh Percy, who had arrived in Lexington with reinforcements for the retreat back to Boston, wrote to a fellow officer about the rebels, "I never believed, I confess, that they w[oul]d have attacked the King's troops, or have had the perseverance I found in them yesterday." He warned, "Whoever looks upon them as an irregular mob, will find himself much mistaken." The battles that day taught Percy that it wasn't just Boston who had stubborn and determined rebels—the countryside did, too. Plenty of them. The Revolutionary War had begun, and it hadn't started well for the Crown. Worse for Gage, the redcoats would foolishly abandon the high ground on which they now rested. It would cost them in blood.[100]

## FROM PAST TO PRESENT

### CAMBRIDGE POWDER HOUSE

*You've got a bit of a trip ahead of you if you're committed to seeing the powder house, which is in Somerville today. If you travel by subway from downtown Boston, you'll take it to Davis Square. From there, it's a ten-minute walk. This journey will give you a tiny feeling for the stamina soldiers needed to march this far out of town. Around the Powder House today are homes and Tufts University, but this land was sparsely developed in 1774. You'll see the powder house at the top of a small hill. It's a humble structure amidst a quiet park and an idyllic place to reflect on the lessons Gage could have learned from his first powder raid.*

The ransacked powder house, tucked away at the top of Powder House Square in Somerville. *Public domain.*

## PAUL REVERE HOUSE

*It is amazing that this structure still stands today, as it was old when Paul Revere bought it. He purchased the wooden house in 1770, when it was nearly ninety years old. After he moved out, it served as a tenement home and also had shops on the bottom floor. Today, it has been thankfully restored to a museum and is one of the most popular stops on the Freedom Trail. The museum grants you access to the first two floors of the house, the ones where Revere likely spent most of his time. You'll get a crowded feeling immediately, not only because of all of the visitors, but also because it is a small house, made more cramped by the low ceilings and exposed wood. Some of the house's material is original, including two doors, some window frames and part of the flooring. Picture living there with your spouse, mother and several of your children, as Revere did, and you'll get a sense of why he loved taverns so much.*

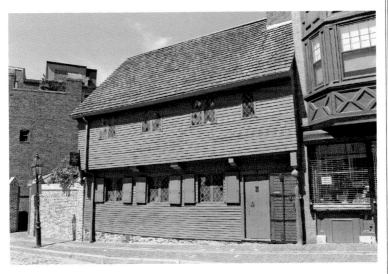

The Paul Revere House in the North End. *Photograph by the author.*

## OLD NORTH CHURCH

The Old North Church steeple is visible at the end of the Paul Revere Mall.
*Photograph by the author.*

*Old North Church is on the Freedom Trail and a short walk from Paul Revere's house. It is still an active church and open to visitors. It has large windows throughout, bringing plenty of natural light into the church. But the real star of Old North is outside—the steeple, for both its bells and lore. Those bells, installed in 1745, are the ones Revere rang in his youth when he was part of a bell ringer club and are still rung today by a volunteer organization. As for the steeple, walk to the top of Copp's Hill because you'll get a better sense of how high it was.*

*Also glance across the harbor, to Charlestown, where the message from the bell tower needed to be seen.*

## LEXINGTON COMMON

*To get to Lexington from Boston, it's best to have a car. Paul Revere may have only needed a horse, and you can get there using the subway and a bus, but a car is easiest. The center of Lexington is Lexington Common, a triangular park that commemorates the site of the beginning of the Revolutionary War. There is traffic on all three of its sides, but with its impossibly plush grass and various trees dotting the perimeter, it still manages to be fairly serene. Steps from the Green is Buckman Tavern, a museum today (no drinks served, unfortunately), and just a bit farther away is the Hancock–Clarke House, also a museum. Both close for the winter and keep limited hours other times of the year, so double check their hours of operation before your visit. While visiting the common, it*

can be difficult to imagine the redcoats and the farmers facing off here because the landscape is so different, but it's easier to picture Revere scurrying into Buckman Tavern to grab Hancock's papers before running into the woods to bury them as the redcoats approach.

Lexington Common stretches behind the statue honoring the militia of Lexington. Buckman Tavern is steps to the right (not visible). *Photograph by the author.*

## North Bridge

*Like Lexington, Concord's Revolutionary War sites are best accessed by car, although you can get from Boston to Concord by commuter rail. It's about a two-mile walk from the train station to North Bridge. North Bridge is part of the Minuteman National Historical Park, which also maintains the Battle Road Trail and several of its sites, including where Paul Revere was captured. The North Bridge (not the original, which was torn down in the late eighteenth century) is part of an expansive park tucked off the main road. The bridge spans over the Concord River, small and peaceful, and you may spot a fisherman wading along the banks or kayakers. Be sure to cross the bridge and look back across the river. That was the view the colonists had before both sides began shooting.*

Concord's North Bridge from the vantage point of the militia. Across the river stood the redcoats. *Photograph by the author.*

# 7

# THE BATTLE FOR BOSTON

*Key Player: Benjamin Church, a Peculiar Doctor*

Paul Revere and Joseph Warren sat stunned. Why would any rebel want to venture into Boston right after the Battles of Lexington and Concord? It was a suicide mission. Yet Dr. Benjamin Church seemed intent on it. Revere, Church and Warren, along with other leading rebels, were gathered in Cambridge rehashing the details of the battles. That afternoon, Church was making quite a spectacle of himself. Church had shown a bloody stocking of his to Revere, as evidence of being in the middle of the previous day's fighting. According to Revere, the blood "had spirted on him from a Man who was killed near" Church, who was "urging the militia on." Revere thought that if a man would put his life in danger for a cause, "he must be a Friend to that cause." But traveling to Boston didn't make sense. Any rebel leader found there would certainly be captured.[101]

Despite the dangers, Church stated that he was going into Boston. Revere said this bold proclamation, "Set them all a staring." Warren, in particular, was incredulous. He asked, "Are you serious, Dr. Church? They will Hang you if they catch you in Boston." Church was deadly serious and said he was "determined to go." Warren, who "had not the greatest affection for" Church, according to Revere, decided that if Church was going to travel to Boston, he should make himself useful. Warren sent Church with a note asking for medical supplies for captured, wounded British officers. With that, Warren was done worrying about Church. Warren was a man on a mission.[102]

Almost immediately after the Battles of Lexington and Concord, the rebels, especially Warren, collected statements from those who'd been there. Nearly all of them claimed that the British fired on the colonists first, including one from Captain John Parker of Lexington, who stated that after ordering his militia to disperse and not to fire, the redcoats "rushed furiously, fired upon and killed Eight of our party, without receiving any Provocation therefor from us." Rebel leaders wanted their versions of the battles to reach London before Gage's potentially contradictory accounts. For years, the rebels had known how important it was to shape people's impressions of an event—recall Revere's depiction of the Boston Massacre—and they wanted their message heard first. While Warren was feverishly working on his account, so was Gage, who thought that because he controlled Boston Harbor he had an advantage in this public-relations battle. Gage planned to send off his versions and then shut down the harbor, prohibiting colonists from sharing their account. That would've been a fine plan if the rebels had been incapable of improvisational thinking.[103]

There was lots of available Massachusetts coastline, and the rebels went north to Salem. They recruited Captain John Derby to take their letters to England aboard his schooner, *Quero*. Derby smartly had his ship traveling in ballast—without any cargo—so it could travel much faster than Gage's sluggish ship, which was weighed down with goods. Derby departed from Salem on Saturday, April 29, four days after Gage's letters left Boston. Gage was none the wiser. Derby and his *Quero* did exactly what Warren needed them to do: get to London first. They beat Gage's ship by an incredible twelve days. Unfortunately for Gage, until his ship arrived, the only account circulating in London was that of the colonists, who told of the regulars firing uncontrollably on a small number of British subjects in Lexington and getting their bayonets handed to them in Concord. When Gage's eagerly awaited accounts finally arrived, they only confirmed that what people in London had hoped were exaggerated accounts were actually true. Hutchinson, for one, was beside himself. Already out of place in London and fretting about his homeland, he wrote in his diary that Gage's accounts provided "little comfort" because they were "much the same with what D[e]rby brought."[104]

# THE SIEGE OF BOSTON

Immediately after the Battles of Lexington and Concord, Gage wanted to control not only the information that went in and out of Boston but also the people. Gage built fortifications on the Neck of Boston and prevented people from leaving or bringing in supplies without his permission. This would prove to be an ineffective tactic because the rebels—who were busy recruiting an army—responded with a barricade of their own. The men composing this new army were different than militia members, who were required to serve but only temporarily. These soldiers were called provincials and volunteered to serve for a designated period of time, typically nine to twelve months. The provincials surrounded Boston and dug reinforcements on the other side of the Boston Neck. Eventually, over fifteen thousand provincials guarded these barricades. With that, Boston was under siege.

The town essentially became an island, trapping the British redcoats, Loyalists and a handful of rebels inside the garrisoned town. Life was grim in Boston during the siege. With several thousand British soldiers occupying Boston, there was a demand for resources that supply could not match. British soldiers frequently tore down homes, bridges and fences for fuel. Fresh food was scarce, and as the laws of supply and demand dictate, the cost of food was very expensive. With a diet devoid of necessary protein and nutrients, inhabitants in Boston were dying at an alarming rate, especially

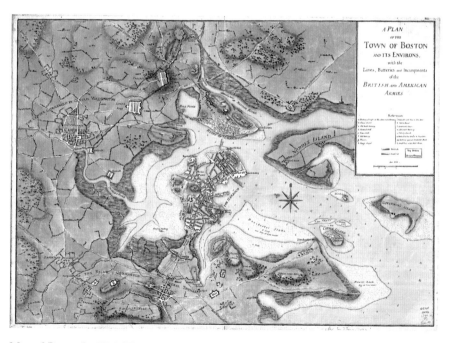

Map of Boston in 1776. The redcoat occupation of Boston extended to the Neck, while provincial troops barricaded the other side. North of Boston is Charlestown, and east of the Neck is Dorchester Heights. *Library of Congress, Geography and Map Division.*

among the poor and elderly. Dysentery was a chief killer, with Gage reporting that "our Hospitals have been very crowded for some time, by the Dissentry." Making this scene even more ghastly was a smallpox epidemic that had broken out in Boston and the surrounding countryside in late 1774. Native New Englanders were more susceptible to catching smallpox than British soldiers, many of whom had already been exposed to the disease in the mother country.[105]

As a result of the funereal scene in Boston, those sympathetic to the rebel cause were trying to flee daily, which made Church's decision to enter into this cesspool all the stranger. Between April and June 1775, as many as ten thousand residents of Boston departed, representing about two-thirds of the town's population. At the same time that rebels fled, about one thousand Loyalists rushed into Boston. They found life to be difficult and intimidating in the countryside and sought the protection of Gage and his soldiers in the safe haven of Boston. Surely that protection would not extend to a rebel like Church when he arrived. Yet Church had an easy time navigating through Boston, even stopping at General Gage's residence and fraternizing with him. Church also took a letter from Paul Revere's wife, Rachel, for him to pass on to Paul. Church voluntarily went in to besieged Boston and communicated with both Loyalists and rebels. It was odd, to say the least.

## BUSY BENJAMIN CHURCH

Regardless of his recent curious behavior, Dr. Benjamin Church was a trusted member of the rebels' inner circles, frequently sitting on committees alongside Adams, Hancock, Otis and Warren. He attended the same schools as many of them—Boston Latin and Harvard College—where he was a classmate of Hancock's. Revere claimed Church "was a high son of Liberty. He frequented all the places where they met, Was incouraged by all the leaders of the Sons of Liberty, and it appeared he was respected by them." Church was witty and used his sharp literary mind to write political satires, frequently poking fun at British policies. He was even given the honor of being the orator on the third anniversary of the Boston Massacre.[106]

Church was one of the most well-trained doctors in Boston, far surpassing the medical training of Joseph Warren. After apprenticing in Boston, Church bolstered his medical knowledge by studying in England. Church also had a bureaucratic mind, evidenced during the war when he worked to get the disparate hospitals in Massachusetts to operate at maximum efficiency. Under Church, rebel soldiers were well cared for—so much so that the Second Continental Congress appointed him director and chief physician of the army hospital. It was a high honor and one that earned him the respect of George Washington, who wasn't overly impressed with many people in Massachusetts.

To balance Church's positive personality traits—competent doctor, sense of humor, gifted writer—he had some personal flaws. He had a lifestyle that he couldn't afford. In 1768, Church built a massive summer home overlooking a large pond in Raynham, Massachusetts. He was constantly strapped for cash during the construction of this country home he didn't need. His shortage of funds didn't preclude him from purchasing another house in 1771, this time in a nice part of Boston. On top of mounting financial trouble, Church also had a mistress whom he had gotten pregnant. He was financially supporting her as well, further increasing his indebtedness. He certainly wasn't gifted with strong judgment.

Those weren't Church's only flaws. The worst of them was his duplicity. Dr. Benjamin Church was a spy who regularly sold rebel secrets to General Gage. The records aren't clear about when Church began his treasonous activities—effective spies don't typically leave behind a pile of evidence—but one biographer believes he began spying as early as 1772. Spies typically turn their coats for financial gain, something Church would have benefited from. Church had actually gone into Boston shortly after the Battles of Lexington and Concord to talk with Gage about the fighting. After the British got trounced at Concord, Church feared that Gage would accuse him of sending British troops into a trap. Church wanted to reassure Gage of his loyalty (ahem) to him, which he successfully seemed to do because Church continued his spy activities after this meeting. And since he was still a trusted member of the rebel leadership, he had access to the most privileged information to sell to Gage.[107]

# BATTLE OF BUNKER HILL

In light of the recent battles and the Siege of Boston, on June 12, 1775, an exasperated Gage issued a bold proclamation declaring martial law in Boston. In it, he castigated the "Incendiaries and Traitors" who have "proceeded into avowed rebellion." To prevent further hostilities and bloodshed, Gage offered a pardon in the king's name to any men who "lay down their arms, and return to the duties of peaceable subjects." The pardon didn't actually extend to all men, for Gage specifically called out John Hancock and Samuel Adams, saying they were excluded from his amnesty because their offenses were too flagrant. Adams seemed to delight in being mentioned, writing from Philadelphia, "Gage has made me respectable by naming me first among those who are to receive no favor from him. I thoroughly despise him and his Proclamation. It is the Subject of Ridicule here."[108]

At the same time that Gage was threatening (and unwittingly pleasing some) rebels, he was also pleading with Lord Dartmouth for more troops. Gage believed another battle could soon break out, and he was beginning to understand the provincials' ability and determination to fight. He predicted that "to carry on a war with effect against this country…not less than 15,000 men should be employed," which was more than double the amount of troops he currently had. Dartmouth was dubious about Gage's claim and slow to send reinforcements. Those in London had not yet realized the type of fighting the rebels could mount. And that was partly the fault of Gage who, for years, had whitewashed his accounts of the struggles between rebels and soldiers.[109]

Both the provincials and Gage knew that the two elevations surrounding Boston were the key to taking control of the town: Dorchester Heights and Bunker Hill in Charlestown. Charlestown was a small town across the harbor from Boston with a population of about two to three thousand inhabitants. Like Boston, it was a hilly town with two notable rises: Bunker Hill, about 110 feet tall, and Breed's Hill, about 60 to 70 feet tall. With armed conflict now in Massachusetts, Gage knew he should grab hold of the high ground of Charlestown. He ordered all of Charlestown's residents to evacuate so they wouldn't interfere with his efforts. They complied, but Gage still did not act. The colonists didn't suffer such delays.

On June 16 around midnight, several hundred provincials under Colonel William Prescott marched to Charlestown and built a quadrangular redoubt, or fort, that was about five to six feet high. There was no moon that night, which was both a blessing and a curse. The darkness minimized the provincials' chance of being spotted by the British while constructing the fortifications, but they also couldn't see well enough to realize that they were building their fort on a hill that wasn't Bunker Hill. They noticed their error around dawn when they could finally see the taller hill behind them and were horrified by their mistake. Fortifications on top of Bunker Hill would have been a defensive move. But putting the fort on Breed's Hill made theirs an offensive position. Breed's was close enough for provincial cannons to reach Boston's North End and Boston Harbor, where the British naval ships patrolled.

Early the next morning, on June 17, 1775, the British saw the provincials' fort and knew they needed to attack. General William Howe would lead. Howe had arrived in Boston a month earlier to help Gage, in whom many in London had lost faith. Howe was no stranger to the colonists, having fought alongside them during the French and Indian War. Before his attack, Howe wanted to frighten and intimidate the provincials and fired cannons for several hours at Breed's Hill and ordered his soldiers to burn down Charlestown's evacuated buildings. Howe then planned to launch a frontal assault around three o'clock that afternoon, but he overlooked two crucial circumstances: the landscape of Breed's Hill and the weather. The grass covering the hill could be as high as the soldiers' waists, making it difficult to effectively or quickly march through, made worse when marching up an incline. Second, the hot June sun and the smoldering town of Charlestown behind the soldiers made their march more laborious. The soldiers' thick wool coats and their heavy packs exacerbated the heat.

The provincials were a little bit more prepared than Howe and his troops, but only a little. First, the provincials had more soldiers than the British. The British had approximately 2,300 to 2,400 regulars, while the provincials had between 2,500 and 3,000 men. Second, the provincials had one of the most inspiring men on the battlefield. Earlier that day, Joseph Warren had showed up at Bunker Hill. The provincials were ecstatic to see him and must have felt more confident knowing he'd be there fighting alongside them. Warren was the only man involved in the highest ranks of Boston's rebel circles to actually fight in the war so far. Despite this boost, the provincials were going to be short on ammunition. Prescott warned his men to conserve gunpowder because their feeble supply would not last in a sustained battle. Rebel muskets had ranges of perhaps 150 feet, so they shouldn't fire until the redcoats were at least within that range. A version of this order has become a part of American legend, with a provincial officer telling his men not "to fire until you see the whites of their eyes." There is no evidence of this order being given that afternoon. Nevertheless, the soldiers were told to wait to fire and aim low, ensuring a bullet would hit the enemy's hips. With that, a battle on Breed's Hill began.

One doesn't need to be a military strategist to know that if your enemy has the high ground, a frontal assault is going to be deadly. And because the redcoats marched up the high ground in lines, they made themselves very

The British cannonading Charlestown before the Battle of Bunker Hill. They fired from warships and Copp's Hill and engulfed Charlestown in flames. *Library of Congress.*

easy targets for the provincials. The provincials were lined three deep in the redoubt, and by taking turns when firing, they were able to keep up a steady line of fire. Reloading a musket took about thirty seconds, so as one man shot, the next in line would fire. Hundreds of British soldiers were shot down and lay dead or wounded on the hill during their first two assaults. The provincials dominated the redcoats in the early stages of the battle; however, their steady firing caused a rapid depletion of gunpowder.

After the slaughter of the first two trips up the hill, Howe wisely changed his strategy. On the third attempt, his men would no longer march up the hill in lines, but in columns. Howe further instructed his soldiers to take off their packs before they went up. The redcoats would have an additional, if gruesome, advantage this time up the hill—the dead or dying bodies of their comrades provided cover from the shooting. With desperation and resolve, the British bravely tried a third assault. The third time was a charm. The rebels ran out of gunpowder during the assault, and the redcoats inched closer to the redoubt. Without gunpowder, and in a futile attempt to slow the redcoats' advance, the provincials threw rocks at the soldiers (which may have worked when mobbing—but not when you're at war). The redcoats forged ahead and climbed into the redoubt. Provincials were left to use their muskets as clubs, swinging them wildly at the redcoats. Knowing it was becoming an increasingly desperate situation, Prescott ordered his men to retreat. The battle was over. The redcoats won and claimed the high ground. They did so at an enormous cost.

The British suffered far more casualties than the colonists in what would be the bloodiest battle of the Revolutionary War: 226 British soldiers were killed and 828 wounded, a casualty rate of close to *half* of their men. Worse than that, the British officers were killed at a much higher rate than ordinary soldiers. Gage somberly wrote, "The number of the killed and wounded is greater than our Force can afford to lose...we have lost some

A confident General William Howe. *The Miriam and Ira D. Wallach Division of Art, Prints and Photographs: Print Collection, New York Public Library.*

extraordinary good Officers." Without intending to do so, the British army had put their officers in grave and visible danger. It was owing to a strange quirk. British private soldiers wore red coats that were made of a different fabric and dye than officers' coats. The coats of privates faded in the sun to a pale pink—not the crimson red that earned the name redcoats. But officers' coats were made with a more expensive fabric, and their coats remained a bright red. This small difference in fabric dramatically influenced the Battle of Bunker Hill, as provincials aimed for the reddest of coats. One brave provincial even acted as a sniper. He stood on a platform that was higher than the rest of his fellow soldiers. He took aim at an officer, fired, handed the musket to a soldier to be reloaded and was handed a fresh musket to repeat the process. He was able to fire at a steady pace for about ten minutes before being picked off by a grenadier. One witness estimated that he had killed more than 20 officers.[110]

The colonists, by contrast, had less than half of the British casualties: 115 men were killed, 270 wounded and 30 captured. But one of those casualties was Joseph Warren. Sadly, Warren was caught in the redoubt when the redcoats climbed in. He was using a sword to fend off British regulars when an officer recognized him. The officer's servant grabbed a pistol and shot Warren in the face. Massachusetts leaders who were in Philadelphia for the Second Continental Congress were shocked and devastated to learn of Warren's death. John Adams wrote, "Our dear Warren has fallen, with

Laurells on his Brows as fresh and blooming as ever graced an Hero." Samuel Adams characteristically consoled himself by bringing it back to the cause. "I sincerely lament the Loss of our truly amiable and worthy Friend," Adams mourned, but "there has scarcely if ever been a Cause so evidently just as that in which he fell so gloriously." Warren's death so early in the war was a tremendous blow to the rebel circles, who would miss his leadership, energy, bravery and dramatic flair.[111]

When those in London learned of what later became known as the Battle of Bunker Hill, they were stunned. No battle during the French and Indian War had come close to matching the casualty total of Bunker Hill. Gage wrote to London a week after the battle and had a reflective tone about him, almost penitent. Mimicking Percy's epiphany after the Battle of Concord, Gage warned Lord Dartmouth that they both may have underestimated the colonists, for "the Rebels are not the despicable Rabble too many have supposed them to be." Gage credited the colonists with a "Military Spirit...joined with an uncommon Degree of Zeal and Enthusiasm." Gage finally now understood that shutting down the rebellion wouldn't be the simple affair he believed it would be when he arrived in Boston with two thousand troops to enforce the Coercive Acts. But it wouldn't matter for him anyway. He learned in September 1775 that he was going to be replaced by William Howe. After being in Boston for a year and a half and suffering through three battles—only one of which was a rout by the British—Gage's time was up. Before he left, Gage offered Dartmouth a final prescient tip. He wrote, "The Conquest of this Country is not easy and can be effected only by Time and Perseverance." He would prove to be both right—subduing the colonists would not be easy—and wrong; despite persevering for eight years, the British would not prevail.[112]

# THE MAKING OF A CONTINENTAL ARMY

As the Battle of Bunker Hill raged in Boston, powerful men in Philadelphia were discussing the Battles of Lexington and Concord. Many delegates of the Second Continental Congress were lukewarm in their support for a war. Continuing their reluctance from the First Continental Congress, conservative delegates believed that the problems of Massachusetts shouldn't become the problems of the rest of the colonies. The Massachusetts delegates argued that the fight against the British

Empire affected everyone, and all colonies should contribute manpower. Massachusetts proposed raising a Continental army, which had never existed in the colonies before, given their fear of standing armies. Some delegates thought that Massachusetts was power hungry, and they expected the colony to nominate one of its own to head up this army.

Delegate John Adams knew that Massachusetts recommending someone from its own colony would only confirm delegates' suspicion about its desire for power. Adams—who liked to put himself in the center of action, even if that wasn't always the reality—claimed to have a solution. According to his autobiography, Adams took the floor of the Congress and spoke glowingly about a man who should be general. John Hancock believed Adams described him. We can only imagine the excitement Hancock momentarily felt to be named to such a prestigious post. Those hopes were dashed when Adams revealed that the man he was praising was actually George Washington. Hancock's face couldn't hide his disappointment. Adams aired Hancock out in his autobiography, claiming that "Mortification and resentment were expressed as forcibly as [Hancock's] Face could exhibit them." When Samuel Adams seconded John's motion, Hancock sulked even more. It resulted in a tense relationship between Hancock and John Adams thereafter. Adams noted that "he never loved me so well after this Event as he had done before."[113]

In the end, George Washington was selected general of the Continental army by the Continental Congress, and he was the right choice. Not only was he taller than nearly every man in any given room—granting him immediate respect—but he also had military experience, unlike Hancock who, according to John Adams, had an "entire Want of Experience in actual Service." As important, Washington was from Virginia, the most populous colony. If Massachusetts could earn Virginia's support for the army and war by nominating one of Virginia's own as its general, it wouldn't take much effort to get other southern colonies on board either. After the selection process was complete, Washington traveled to Massachusetts and arrived in Cambridge on July 2, 1775.[114]

The Virginian George Washington was out of place among many of the men from Massachusetts. *Library of Congress.*

*Left*: Church's ciphered letter. His simple code substituted a letter from the alphabet with a symbol or alternate letter. *Library of Congress.*

*Right*: Henry Knox's size and affability are evident in this portrait, which was completed years after the evacuation of Boston. *National Portrait Gallery, Smithsonian Institution.*

General George Washington, an extremely wealthy and genteel Virginian, was not pleased with what he saw or heard in Massachusetts. He was briefed on the Battle of Bunker Hill and devastated to learn the provincials had lost because they ran out of ammunition. Under his own command, he predicted that "the Regulars would have met with a shameful defeat." (Washington seemed to believe he possessed the power to manifest more gunpowder in the middle of a battle.) Worse than being undersupplied, though, was the undisciplined nature of the men he saw, in whom Washington had little military confidence. Washington described the officers as "the most indifferent kind of People I ever saw" and the soldiers as "an exceeding dirty & nasty people."[115] Meow.

In addition to his dismal troops, in the fall of 1775, the man Washington trusted with the medical care of his soldiers was caught as a spy. Church's treachery was discovered when he foolishly trusted his mistress to pass on a ciphered letter for him. She didn't know how to get the correspondence into the hands of the right people and gave it to her ex-husband, who turned the letter over to the Continental army for investigation. General Washington put two men on the case, and they easily cracked the simple code. In the letter, Church informed a British official about the strength of colonial troops. When questioned, Church denied spying for the British. He said that he was trying to trick the British troops into believing that the colonists had more troops and ammunition than they actually did. Washington saw right through this. If it were not sensitive information, Church would have written the letter in plain, no-need-to-translate English. The colonies had no policy for what to do with a spy—they weren't yet their own country, so officially a treason charge would be against the king—but Washington thought it best to isolate him. Church was imprisoned for the next two years, during which he further embarrassed himself, as he and his father frequently complained about prison life exacerbating his asthma.

While Church was disappointing Washington, one man from Boston, Henry Knox, was impressing him. Knox was a young man, just twenty-five years old, and was tall, husky and quite likeable. Before the war, Knox had a bookstore in Boston where he frequently read books about military tactics and engineering and became a self-taught military strategist. He proved his mettle to Washington when, after the capture of Fort Ticonderoga in upstate New York in May 1775, he and some men took nearly sixty tons of cannons and other weapons through snow and sleet back to Boston. Knox would be rewarded for this capture and transport—Washington later named him the head of artillery for the Continental army. Washington planned to use Knox's cannons to end the siege and finally expunge the British from Boston.

## "REMOVAL OF THE BARBARIANS"

To break the siege, Washington thought the Continental army should attack Boston. He wanted to attack when Boston Harbor was frozen in the winter—limiting the navy's ability to aid the town. Washington's officials, however, advised against this strategy. They didn't believe that their current army could engage in a prolonged battle in Boston. Washington's team instead recommended that they occupy a hill that looked down on Boston, the one-hundred-foot-tall Dorchester Heights. They were surprised that Howe hadn't already secured this strategic location. After the Battle of Bunker Hill, Gage and Howe had, in fact, planned to take Dorchester Heights—even mobilizing two thousand troops for the job. But Gage backed out, believing that the provincial troops who would oppose him were more plentiful than they were. Once again, the colonists beat the British to strategic high ground.

To avoid being spotted, Washington's men transported the cannons up Dorchester Heights at night. Much like the surprise of fortifications sprouting up one morning on Breed's Hill, the British looked up on March 5—the sixth anniversary of the Boston Massacre—to see that Dorchester Heights had been occupied with cannons trained down on Boston and its harbor, capable of blowing it to bits. Howe thought about attacking Dorchester Heights but said the "boisterous" weather prohibited it. "I could promise myself little success by attacking them under all the disadvantages I had to encounter," Howe wrote. Howe wanted to be out of Boston just as much as Washington wanted him out, and the cannons forced the issue. On March 8, Howe sent a letter to Washington agreeing to retreat from Boston and not burn the town down in the process, if his troops were allowed to leave safely. Washington agreed. Approximately one thousand Loyalists and the last of the British troops evacuated Boston on the morning of March 17, 1776, never to return. Samuel Adams proclaimed his joy over "the Removal of the Barbarians from the Capital." Evacuation Day, as it became known, was a triumphant moment for the rebels and Boston. After fifteen months under siege, Boston would never again be occupied by redcoats.[116]

Samuel Adams was giddy with the liberation of Boston but knew that it was not the end of the rebels' struggle. Writing from Philadelphia to the president of the Provincial Congress, Adams believed it "becomes us to rejoice" over the evacuation. His town was finally free of the standing army he had loathed for years. True to Adams's character, though, he gave himself a moment to celebrate before turning his attention to a much bigger and more important concern, one that would top Boston's twelve years of resistance to the mother country: "the Necessity of proclaiming Independency." He and Boston wouldn't have to wait much longer.[117]

# FROM PAST TO PRESENT

## BUNKER HILL BATTLEGROUND

*This site is the last stop on the Freedom Trail and an appropriate place to reflect on the trail's sites and history. A small section of the actual*

The Bunker Hill Monument stands at the top of Breed's Hill. The statue of William Prescott is visible in front of the monument. *Public domain.*

battlefield is fenced off and called Monument Square. Walk to the top of the hill and look down toward the harbor. Wipe away the condominiums and instead picture grass up to your knees, a smoldering town at water's edge and two thousand British redcoats marching toward you. After imagining the redcoats marching up, you can also attempt to feel the close contact fighting in the redoubt and the utter shock and horror you would feel watching Joseph Warren, one of your most committed leaders, fall.

As you walk into the park, you'll see a statue of William Prescott with his sword unsheathed, presumably battling soldiers in the redoubt. If you're feeling adventurous, you can climb to the top of the Bunker Hill monument. At 221 feet tall, with a narrow and winding staircase, it won't appeal to everyone. You'll also find the Bunker Hill lodge behind the monument, which was built in the early twentieth century to house a statue of Joseph Warren. There is also the small Bunker Hill Museum across the street.

## COPP'S HILL BURYING GROUND

Copp's Hill Burying Ground is half a block from Old North Church on the Freedom Trail. It is a massive cemetery that overlooks the water, which made it a strategic location during the siege. The British occupied the hill during the Battle of Bunker Hill and cannonaded Charlestown from here. When you visit, walk to the north side of the cemetery and look for the grave of Daniel Malcom, brother of the tarred and feathered John Malcom. This rebel's headstone was a favorite target for British soldiers, and their bullet holes are still visible on his marker today. Not many well-known people are buried here, but you could visit the tombs of father and son Increase and Cotton Mather, who were famously involved with the Salem Witch Trials. Robert Newman, one of the men to put the signal lanterns in Old North Church, is buried here. Sometimes a black cat can also be seen roaming the graveyard.

Copp's Hill Burying Ground, with Daniel Malcom's headstone in the foreground and Old North Church's steeple in the background. *Photograph by the author.*

## DORCHESTER HEIGHTS

*Today, this elevation is in South Boston, and much like Beacon Hill, it has a lower elevation than it did in the 1770s. There is a quiet park with a tall monument commemorating the site. Walk to the top of the hill and look back at Boston. You'll be able to see why this hill was so important to freeing Boston, as it gave a clear view (and therefore a clear target) of the town in the eighteenth century.*

The monument at the top of Dorchester Heights in South Boston commemorates the evacuation of British troops in March 1776. *Public domain.*

# Epilogue

After the redcoats evacuated Boston, the town barely resembled what it had a year earlier. Boston's population of 15,500 people had plummeted to about 3,500. The rebels who had fled during the siege slowly returned. They may not have suffered the same trials as those who had been trapped in Boston suffered, but the physical damage to their homes, churches and streets was equal. Buildings were in shambles or completely gone; homes had been ransacked and abandoned. Boston would rebuild, but it would take years to restore the town and its population. Many Loyalists also moved after the evacuation—but not back to Boston. They found England and Canada more welcoming.

As Samuel Adams had hoped after British evacuation, the thirteen colonies would declare independence in July 1776. When the Declaration of Independence was first read to the residents of Boston on July 18, 1776, it was done from the balcony of the Old State House. Bostonians were so excited about the declaration that a crowd stormed to the top of the Old State House and ripped down the lion and unicorn in the top corners of the building. The lion and unicorn were symbols of the British Empire—the lion represented England, the unicorn Scotland—and the crowd no longer wanted those symbols up. The mob then burned the lion and unicorn as part of a bonfire on King Street. So Bostonians mobbed when they were upset and when they were free and independent. (Go figure.)

Meanwhile, the Revolutionary War raged on—with the Continental army fighting alongside invaluable French allies—until the colonists finally defeated the British. The war concluded with the signing of the Treaty of Paris in 1783. As Boston recovered from war, it did so with and without some of the people from our story.

# WHERE ARE THEY NOW?

JAMES OTIS JR. In September 1769, Otis got into a fight with a British customs officer at the British Coffee House, a tavern frequented by Loyalists, and without a doubt, Otis got the worse end of the fight he'd picked. His beating severely affected his mental state—which wasn't stable to begin with—and Otis would never be the same psychologically, nor would his involvement in the rebel cause. His life ended in the rarest of circumstances. In 1783, James Otis was struck dead by a bolt of lightning.

SAMUEL ADAMS. After the troops evacuated, Adams remained in politics for two more decades. He sat on the Massachusetts Constitutional Convention of 1780, but he was not a part of the Constitutional Convention in Philadelphia. While he was initially reluctant to support the U.S. Constitution, Adams eventually did, as long as a Bill of Rights was added. In the 1790s, Samuel Adams served for a few years as governor of Massachusetts. In 1797, Adams received the fifth most votes for U.S. president, but he retired that same year from public life and as governor. In retirement, he could be seen walking around Boston (still dressed like a mess, but this time because his tricornered hat was out of fashion), representing a different time and people. He died in 1803 at the age of eighty-one.

THOMAS HUTCHINSON. Hutchinson left for London in June 1774, believing he would return to Boston once order had been restored. In London, he had an audience with King George III, who wanted Hutchinson's insider perspective on the people of Massachusetts. Hutchinson believed he could help to broker a reconciliation between the Crown and colonies but eventually realized that was impossible. In July 1779, Hutchinson heard that a law in Massachusetts formally banished him from Massachusetts forever. He died of a stroke less than a year later, in 1780, never having returned to his homeland.

JOHN HANCOCK. As president of the Second Continental Congress, Hancock had the privilege of being the first person to sign the Declaration of Independence. That was as high as his national star would rise, but Massachusetts would continue to love him. In 1780, Hancock became the first elected governor of Massachusetts, and he served several one-year terms before dying in office in 1793 at the age of fifty-six. His lieutenant governor, Samuel Adams, took over as governor.

EBENEZER RICHARDSON. After shooting Christopher Snider, Boston crowds tried twice to hang Richardson. He eventually stood trial and pleaded self-defense but was convicted of murder. Richardson was released after spending two years in jail and paying a small fee. He later received a royal pardon for his murder of Snider.

RICHARD CLARKE. Clarke moved to London in 1775 and lived with his son-in-law, John Singleton Copley, for the remainder of his life. While in London, he was part of a club comprising other Loyalists who had left the colonies. They met once a week and shared dinner together, likely swapping stories about their mistreatment during the Revolution. He died in 1795 at the age of eighty-three.

JOHN SINGLETON COPLEY. Despite painting many of Boston's most fervent rebels, Copley identified as a Loyalist in 1774. Shortly thereafter, he left his family behind in Boston, sailed for London and did not come back. He was eventually elected to the Royal Academy of Art and had his paintings commissioned by King George III. Ironically, Copley is often considered an American artist sympathetic to the rebel cause, even having Copley Square in Boston's Back Bay bear his name and a statue of him.

JOHN ADAMS. A fairly minor character in Boston's rebellion in the 1760s and early 1770s, John Adams became one of the most successful national politicians from Massachusetts, serving as vice president under George Washington. He also served one term as the second president of the United States and was the only Federalist to assume that office. After leaving political office, Adams wrote his autobiography, which can be petty and self-serving, written with posterity in mind.

PAUL REVERE. Of the sixteen (!) children Paul had in his life, his son born in 1777 carried a special name, Joseph Warren Revere, in honor of Revere's fallen friend in the Battle of Bunker Hill. During the Revolutionary War, Paul Revere served in the Continental army, commanding a disastrous campaign in Penobscot Bay, Maine. In the 1780s, he fortunately returned to his silver making and eventually expanded to casting bells and creating copper sheets—his work would top the new Massachusetts State House dome and be added to the USS *Constitution*. At the beginning of the nineteenth century, Revere founded a copper company that still exists in name today. Revere died in 1818, at the age of eighty-three.

HENRY KNOX. Knox had a meteoric rise under the watch of George Washington, becoming the first president's first secretary of war. When the U.S. Army opened an artillery camp in Kentucky in 1918, it was named for Henry Knox, today known as Fort Knox.

THOMAS GAGE. General Gage returned to London in October 1775, never continuing his military activities to the same degree as he did in America. He would remain in England the rest of his life, dying in 1787.

BENJAMIN CHURCH. The uncertainty of what to do with Benjamin Church continued for two more years as he was moved around from jail to jail. In 1777, his wife took their children and left for London, where she convinced the Crown that she deserved an annual pension for her husband's service. In January 1778, Massachusetts leaders voted to permit Benjamin Church to leave the colonies, as long as he didn't return. He wouldn't. His ship set sail one month later, bound for Martinique. The ship and Church were lost at sea.

# FROM PAST TO PRESENT

## GRANARY BURYING GROUND

*The Granary Burying Ground is an American Revolution celebrity burying ground where you'll find the headstones of Samuel Adams, John Hancock, Paul Revere and James Otis. The headstones of Otis and Adams anchor the front corners of the graveyard. The headstone of Revere will underwhelm you, while that of Hancock will make you smile. It suits him perfectly because it is a large and conspicuous structure—his face is even engraved at the top. You'll also see the headstones of the victims of the Boston Massacre and young Christopher Snider. The burying ground is on the Freedom Trail and centrally located, so it's a must-visit while in Boston.*

The celebrity-filled Granary Burying Ground in downtown Boston. *Photograph by the author.*

# Notes

## Chapter 1

1. Nathaniel B. Shurtleff, *A Topographical and Historical Description of Boston* (Boston: Boston City Council, 1871), 61.
2. Douglass Adair and John A. Schutz, eds., *Peter Oliver's Origin & Progress of the American Revolution: A Tory View* (San Marino, CA: Huntington Library, 1961), 46.
3. Edmund S. Morgan, ed., *Prologue to Revolution: Sources and Documents on the Stamp Act Crisis, 1764–1766* (Chapel Hill: University of North Carolina Press, 1959), 4.
4. Ibid., 18.
5. Harry Alonzo Cushing, ed., *Writings of Samuel Adams*, vol. 1, *1764–1769* (New York: G.P. Putnam's Sons, 1904), 5.
6. Adair and Schutz, *Origin & Progress of the American Revolution*, 41.
7. James Otis, *Rights of the British Colonies Asserted and Proved* (London, 1764), Gale: Eighteenth Century Collections Online, 99.

## Chapter 2

8. Cushing, *Writings of Samuel Adams*, 1:8–9, 10.
9. John W. Tyler and Elizabeth Dubrulle, eds., *Correspondence of Thomas Hutchinson*, vol. 1, *1740–1766* (Boston: Colonial Society of Massachusetts, 2014), 277.

10. Adair and Schutz, *Origin & Progress of the American Revolution*, 28.

11. Tyler and Dubrulle, *Correspondence of Thomas Hutchinson*, 300.

12. Peter Orlando Hutchinson, *Diary and Letters of His Excellency Thomas Hutchinson, Esq.* (New York: Burt Franklin, 1971), 1:457.

13. Cushing, *Writings of Samuel Adams*, vol. 2, *1770–1773* (New York: G.P. Putnam's Sons, 1906), 201.

14. Morgan, *Prologue to Revolution*, 107; Tyler and Dubrulle, *Correspondence of Thomas Hutchinson*, 279.

15. Cushing, *Writings of Samuel Adams*, 2:201; Clarence Edwin Carter, ed., *Correspondence of General Thomas Gage with the Secretaries of State*, vol. 1, *1763–1775* (Hamden, CT: Archon Books, 1969), 67.

16. Tyler and Dubrulle, *Correspondence of Thomas Hutchinson*, 287.

17. Ibid., 290, 291, 296–97.

18. Colin Nicolson, ed., *Papers of Francis Bernard, Governor of Colonial Massachusetts, 1760–1769*, vol. 2 (Boston: Colonial Society of Massachusetts, 2012), 323.

19. Tyler and Dubrulle, *Correspondence of Thomas Hutchinson*, 318–22.

20. Ibid., 293; Cushing, *Writings of Samuel Adams*, 1:59–60.

21. Samuel Eliot Morison, ed., *Sources & Documents Illustrating the American Revolution 1764–1788 and the Formation of the Federal Constitution*, 2nd ed. (London: Oxford University Press, 1970), 33.

22. Nicolson, *Papers of Francis Bernard*, 2:397.

23. Cushing, *Writings of Samuel Adams*, 1:109.

24. Morgan, *Prologue to Revolution*, 155; Adair and Schutz, *Origin & Progress of the American Revolution*, 56.

25. Tyler and Dubrulle, *Correspondence of Thomas Hutchinson*, 428.

26. Ibid., 450.

## CHAPTER 3

27. Adair and Schutz, *Origin & Progress of the American Revolution*, 67.

28. Yale Avalon Online, "Great Britain: Parliament—The Townshend Act, November 20, 1767," http://avalon.law.yale.edu/18th_century/townsend_act_1767.asp.

29. Cushing, *Writings of Samuel Adams*, 1:136–38, 165.

30. Ibid., 185–86.

31. Neil L. York, *Boston Massacre: A History with Documents*, 57.

32. Cushing, *Writings of Samuel Adams*, 1:232–36.

33. York, *Boston Massacre*, 61.

34. Nicolson, *Papers of Francis Bernard*, vol. 4 (Boston: Colonial Society of Massachusetts, 2015), 185.

35. Adair and Schutz, *Origin & Progress of the American Revolution*, 69–70; Cushing, *Writings of Samuel Adams*, 1:238.

36. Carter, *Correspondence of Gage*, 220; Kinvin Wroth and Hiller B. Zobel, eds., *Legal Papers of John Adams*, vol. 2 (Cambridge, MA: Belknap Press of Harvard University Press, 1965), 197.

37. York, *Boston Massacre*, 61–63.

38. Paul D. Brandes, *John Hancock's Life and Speeches: A Personalized Vision of the American Revolution, 1763–1793* (Lanham, MD: Scarecrow Press, 1996), 215; Cushing, *Writings of Samuel Adams*, 1:269.

39. Carter, *Correspondence of Gage*, 203.

40. Oliver Morton Dickerson, ed., *Boston Under Military Rule, 1768–1769, As Revealed in a Journal of the Times* (New York: Da Capo Press, 1970), 2.

41. Ibid., 8.

42. Ibid.

43. Ibid., 9.

44. Carter, *Correspondence of Gage*, 203.

45. Ibid.

## Chapter 4

46. Dickerson, *Boston Under Military Rule*, 17.

47. Carter, *Correspondence of Gage*, 249; York, *Boston Massacre*, 147–48.

48. Cushing, *Writings of Samuel Adams*, 1:258, 392; Dickerson, *Boston Under Military Rule*, 19, 28.

49. Cushing, *Writings of Samuel Adams*, 1:351, 353.

50. Bernard Bailyn, *Ordeal of Thomas Hutchinson*, 132.

51. York, *Boston Massacre*, 85.

52. Due to the inconsistent and sometimes nonexistent records of the eighteenth century, Christopher Snider's surname is sometimes spelled Seider, and some accounts claim he was twelve years old when he was killed.

53. Samuel A. Forman, *Dr. Joseph Warren: The Boston Tea Party, Bunker Hill, and the Birth of American Liberty* (Gretna, LA: Pelican Publishing Company, 2012), 185–88. Forman speculates that Warren fathered a child with Sally Edwards, even as he was engaged to Mercy Scollay.

54. K.G. Davies, *Documents of the American Revolution, 1770–1783*, vol. 2 (Shannon: Irish University Press, 1972), 51; *Boston Gazette and Country Journal*, February 26, 1770, Massachusetts Historical Society Online, Annotated Newspapers of Harbottle Dorr Jr.

55. York, *Boston Massacre*, 110.

56. Ibid., 136, 148–49.

57. Ibid., 149; Cushing, *Writings of Samuel Adams*, 2:86.

58. Wroth and Zobel, *Legal Papers of John Adams*, 3:266.

59. York, *Boston Massacre*, 111.

60. Ibid., 153, 179.

61. Davies, *Documents of the American Revolution*, 2:51.

62. Carter, *Correspondence of Gage*, 251, 264.

63. Cushing, *Writings of Samuel Adams*, 2:79.

64. Wroth and Zobel *Legal Papers of John Adams*, 3:259; York, *Boston Massacre*, 193.

65. York, *Boston Massacre*, 185.

66. Ibid., 202–03.

## CHAPTER 5

67. *Copy of Letters Sent to Great-Britain by His Excellency Thomas Hutchinson, the Hon. Andrew Oliver, and Several Other Persons* (n.p., 1769; rpr., Project Gutenberg, 2015) EBook #48819; Cushing, *Writings of Samuel Adams*, vol. 3, *1773–1777* (New York: G.P. Putnam's Sons, 1907), 44.

68. Davies, *Documents of the American Revolution, 1770–1783*, vol. 3 (Shannon: Irish University Press, 1973), 103.

69. Ibid., 206, 218.

70. *Boston Gazette, and Country Journal*, November 8, 1773, Massachusetts Historical Society Online, Annotated Newspapers of Harbottle Dorr Jr.

71. Ibid.

72. Davies, *Documents of the American Revolution, 1770–1783*, vol. 6 (Shannon: Irish University Press, 1974), 248.

73. Ibid., 249.

74. *Boston Gazette, and Country Journal*, December 13, 1773, Massachusetts Historical Society Online, The Annotated Newspapers of Harbottle Dorr Jr.

75. Cushing, *Writings of Samuel Adams*, 3:73–74.

76. Ibid., 72.

77. For more about the Boston Tea Party participants, including their age, see ch. 6 of Benjamin L. Carp, *Defiance of the Patriots: The Boston Tea Party and the Making of America* (New Haven, CT: Yale University Press, 2010).

78. Adair and Schutz, *Origin & Progress of the American Revolution*, 98.

79. Cushing, *Writings of Samuel Adams*, 3:110.

80. Carter, *Correspondence of Gage*, 380.

81. Davies, *Documents of the American Revolution, 1770–1783*, vol. 8 (Dublin: Ireland University Press, 1975), 90.

82. Cushing, *Writings of Samuel Adams*, 3:137, 142.

83. Shurtleff, *Topographical and Historical Description of Boston*, 611.

## CHAPTER 6

84. Cushing, *Writings of Samuel Adams*, 3:156.

85. Carter, *Correspondence of Gage*, 394.

86. Cushing, *Writings of Samuel Adams*, 3:206.

87. Ibid.

88. Davies, *Documents of the American Revolution, 1770–1783*, vol. 9 (Dublin: Irish University Press, 1975), 39.

89. Edmund S. Morgan, ed., *Paul Revere's Three Accounts of His Famous Ride* (Boston: A Revolutionary War Bicentennial Commission and Massachusetts Historical Society Publication, 1967), "The Deposition: Corrected Copy."

90. Ibid.

91. Ibid.

92. Ibid.

93. Ibid.

94. Ibid.

95. Davies, *Documents of the American Revolution*, 9:103.

96. Morgan, *Paul Revere's Three Accounts*, "The Deposition: Corrected Copy."

97. Eric Bruun and Jay Crosby, *Our Nation's Archive: The History of the United States in Documents* (New York: Black Dog & Leventhal Publishers, 1999), 120.

98. Carter, *Correspondence of Gage*, 396; Davies, *Documents of the American Revolution*, 9:104.

99. Carter, *Correspondence of Gage*, 396.

100. Charles Knowles Bolton, *Letters of Hugh Earl Percy from Boston and New York, 1774–1776* (Boston: Charles E. Goodspeed, 1902), 52–53.

# CHAPTER 7

101. Morgan, *Paul Revere's Three Accounts*, Letter to Jeremy Belknap.

102. Ibid.

103. Ezra Ripley, *A History of the Fight at Concord on the 19ᵗʰ of April, 1775* (Concord, MA: Allen & Atwill, 1827), 55.

104. Hutchinson, *Diary and Letters of His Excellency Thomas Hutchinson*, 466.

105. Carter, *Correspondence of Gage*, 416.

106. Morgan, *Paul Revere's Three Accounts*, Letter to Jeremy Belknap.

107. John A. Nagy, *Dr. Benjamin Church, Spy: A Case of Espionage on the Eve of the American Revolution* (Yardley, PA: Westholme Publishing, 2013), 160.

108. "Proclamation by General Thomas Gage, June 12, 1775," Library of Congress Online, Teachers Classroom Materials; Cushing, *Writings of Samuel Adams*, 3:221.

109. Davies, *Documents of the American Revolution*, 9:170.

110. Carter, *Correspondence of Gage*, 407.

111. *Warren-Adams Letters: Being chiefly a correspondence among John Adams, Samuel Adams, and James Warren*, vol. 1, *1743–1777* (Boston: Massachusetts Historical Society, 1917), 66, 70.

112. Carter, *Correspondence of Gage*, 407.

113. John Adams Autobiography (part 1, 1776, sheet 21 of 53) Adams Family Papers: An Electronic Archive, Massachusetts Historical Society, http://www.masshist.org/digitaladams.

114. John Adams Autobiography (part 1, sheet 20 of 53).

115. W.W. Abbot, ed., *Papers of George Washington*, Revolutionary War Series, vol. 1, June-September 1775 (Charlottesville: University Press of Virginia, 1983) 335–36.

116. Davies, *Documents of the American Revolution*, vol. 12 (Dublin: Ireland University Press, 1976), 273.

117. *Warren-Adams Letters*, 224.

# Suggested Reading

Adair, Douglass, and John A. Schutz, eds. *Peter Oliver's Origin & Progress of the American Revolution: A Tory View*. San Marino, CA: Huntington Library, 1961.

Allison, Robert J. *A Short History of Boston*. Beverly, MA: Commonwealth Editions, 2004.

Anderson, Fred. *Crucible of War: The Seven Years' War and the Fate of Empire in British North America, 1754–1766*. New York: Alfred A. Knopf, 2000.

———. *A People's Army: Massachusetts Soldiers and Society in the Seven Years' War*. Chapel Hill: University of North Carolina Press, 1984.

Archer, Richard. *As If an Enemy's Country: The British Occupation of Boston and the Origins of the Revolution*. New York: Oxford University Press, 2010.

Bahne, Charles. *The Complete Guide to Boston's Freedom Trail*. 4th ed. Cambridge, MA: Newtowne Publishing, 2013.

Bailyn, Bernard. *The Ideological Origins of the American Revolution*. Cambridge, MA: Belknap Press of Harvard University Press, 1967.

———. *The Ordeal of Thomas Hutchinson*. Cambridge, MA: Belknap Press of Harvard University Press, 1974.

Beeman, Richard R. *Our Lives, Our Fortunes, and Our Sacred Honor: The Forging of American Independence, 1774–1776*. New York: Basic Books, 2013.

Bell, J.L. *Boston 1775* (blog). http://boston1775.blogspot.com.

Bunker, Nick. *An Empire on the Edge: How Britain Came to Fight America*. New York: Alfred A. Knopf, 2014.

Carp, Benjamin L. *Defiance of the Patriots: The Boston Tea Party and the Making of America*. New Haven, CT: Yale University Press, 2010.

Carr, Jacqueline. *After the Siege: A Social History of Boston, 1775–1800*. Boston: Northeastern University Press, 2005.

Commager, Henry Steele, and Richard B. Norris, eds. *The Spirit of Seventy-Six: The Story of the American Revolution as Told by Participants*. New York: Harper & Row Publishers, 1958, 1967.

Conroy, David W. *In Public Houses: Drink & Revolution of Authority in Colonial Massachusetts*. Chapel Hill: University of North Carolina Press, 1995.

Federal Writers' Project. *The WPA Guide to Massachusetts*. New York: Pantheon Books, 1983.

Fenn, Elizabeth A. *Pox Americana: The Great Smallpox Epidemic of 1775–1782*. New York: Hill and Wang, 2001.

Fischer, David Hackett. *Paul Revere's Ride*. New York: Oxford University Press, 1994.

Forbes, Esther. *Paul Revere and the World He Lived In*. Boston: Houghton Mifflin Company, 1942.

Fowler, William M., Jr. *Samuel Adams: Radical Puritan*. Edited by Oscar Handlin. New York: Addison-Wesley Educational Publishers Inc., 1997.

Kay, Jane Holtz. *Lost Boston*. Expanded and updated ed. Amherst: University of Massachusetts Press, 2006.

Krieger, Alex, and David Cobb, eds. *Mapping Boston*. Cambridge, MA: MIT Press, 1999.

Maier, Pauline. *From Resistance to Revolution: Colonial Radicals and the Development of American Opposition to Britain, 1765–1776*. New York: W.W. Norton, 1991.

———. *The Old Revolutionaries: Political Lives in the Age of Samuel Adams*. New York: Alfred A. Knopf, 1980.

Morgan, Edmund S. *The Birth of the Republic, 1763–1789*. 4th ed. Chicago: University of Chicago Press, 2013.

Morgan, Edmund S., and Helen M. Morgan. *The Stamp Act Crisis: The Prologue to Revolution*. 2nd ed. Chapel Hill: University of North Carolina Press, 1995.

Nagy, John A. *Dr. Benjamin Church, Spy: A Case of Espionage on the Eve of the American Revolution*. Yardley, PA: Westholme Publishing, 2013.

Nelson, James L. *With Fire and Sword: The Battle of Bunker Hill and the Beginning of the American Revolution*. New York: Thomas Dunne Books, 2011.

Philbrick, Nathaniel. *Bunker Hill: A City, a Siege, a Revolution*. New York: Penguin Books, 2014.

Stoll, Ira. *Samuel Adams: A Life*. New York: Free Press, 2008.

Taylor, Alan. *American Colonies*. New York: Penguin Books, 2001.

————. *Colonial America: A Very Short Introduction*. New York: Oxford University Press, 2012.

Thwing, Annie Haven. *The Crooked and Narrow Streets of the Town of Boston, 1633–1822*. Boston: Marshall Jones Co., 1920.

Tourtellot, Arthur B. *Lexington and Concord: The Beginning of the War of the American Revolution*. New York: W.W. Norton & Company, 1959.

Unger, Harlow Giles. *John Hancock: Merchant King and American Patriot*. Edison, NJ: Castle Books, 2005.

Wood, Gordon S. *The American Revolution: A History*. New York: Modern Library, 2002.

York, Neil L. *The Boston Massacre: A History with Documents*. New York: Routledge, Taylor & Francis Group, 2010.

Young, Alfred F. *Liberty Tree: Ordinary People and the American Revolution*. New York: New York University Press, 2006.

————. *The Shoemaker and the Tea Party: Memory and the American Revolution*. Boston: Beacon Press, 1999.

Zobel, Hiller R. *The Boston Massacre*. New York: W.W. Norton, 1970.

# INDEX

# About the Author

 rooke Barbier received her PhD in American history from Boston College. In 2013, she founded Ye Olde Tavern Tours, offering spirited tours of Boston's Freedom Trail. When she's not talking about history, she's watching baseball, especially the Red Sox. A native of San Diego, she has resided in Boston for fifteen years.